Good BEER GUIDE

TO
PRAGUE
AND THE
CZECH
REPUBLIC

Graham Lees

BOOKS

Author: Graham Lees
Design: Rob Howells
Maps: Perrott Cartographics, Machynlleth
Typeset by T&O Graphics, Broome, Bungay, Suffolk
Printed by WSOY, Finland

Published by CAMRA Books, Campaign for Real Ale, 230
Hatfield Road, St Albans AL1 4LW
ISBN 1 85249 122 1
Copyright CAMRA Books 1996

CONTENTS

Page

ACKNOWLEDGEMENTS

My grateful thanks to Dave Cunningham and Peter Dyer for their tireless translations of Czech newspapers and documents and, with Neil Kellett, for helping to unravel Prague; Jarmila Hrabalova who prefers wine but became a beer expert while interpreting her way round breweries on my behalf; Denis Cox and the PIVEX trade fair staff in Brno; Roger Protz, Jo Bates and Richard Smith at CAMRA; and the numerous brewers and brewing staff across the Czech Republic who generously opened their doors to me.

Graham Lees
Manchester

April 24, 1996

INTRODUCTION

W E ALWAYS knew the Czechs had a taste for beer. For many years this century they have been at the top of the world's beer-drinking league, vying with either the Germans, Danes, or Belgians for the crown. It was a Czech town which added the word Pilsner to the world's beer-drinking vocabulary, and Bohemia has one of the longest brewing histories in Europe. Bohemians were exporting hops for beer-making long before William the Conqueror invaded England.

But for almost fifty years until the dawn of the 1990s, a veil had been drawn over this beautiful part of central Europe and those of us living west of the Iron Curtain had little idea exactly what was brewing in the country now called the Czech Republic.

This book sets out to draw back the veil to reveal the delights of the Czech brewhouse and pub, both for salivating armchair travellers and especially for those adventurous souls ready to head for one of Europe's most beautiful and beery regions.

They will find that the Czech brew kettle is still gleaming and steaming, the hop fields still blooming, and the smoky beer halls of Prague which were known to such central European intellectual luminaries as Einstein, Kafka, Smetana and Dvorak, are still humming with well-lubricated chatter. They will discover rural pubs clinging to the sides of castles and many more clustered round the ancient arcaded squares of dozens of medieval villages and towns where time seems to have stood still. In fact, the Czechs probably have more castles per capita than anywhere else – about 1,800 – and dozens are detailed in this book where they dovetail with an inviting brewery town or recommended pub.

The fall of Communism, the rise of capitalism and the ascendancy of Prague as one of the top ten most-visited cities of Europe have fundamentally changed Czechs and their country. It is still poor by western standards – with beer as cheap as 17 pence a pint in some places. Life is still a struggle for many people but they now have more material things to do with their spare cash. And after an initial drinking spree to celebrate the end of Communism, which saw beer sales temporarily rocket, consumption is now starting to drop, ironically as virtually every brewery in the country invests in new technology to increase production.

Even so, in 1994 Czechs drank 283 pints of beer per head of population, out in front of the Germans' 251, the Danes' 225 and the much less thirsty British average of 180. (The Czech Republic figure is much higher than for former Czechoslovakia before it split into two countries in 1993, thus proving that the

Slovaks prefer wine).

It's hardly surprising therefore that this small country of just over ten million people also has more breweries per head of population than anywhere else on earth apart from Germany, in first place, and Belgium, in second. In early 1996, there were about eighty breweries in the Czech Republic. That's a small rise on the tally in 1992 when the sacked Communists' nationalised brewing conglomerates were being broken up and privatised. Several old-established breweries have closed in recent years, but the rise is due to a dozen or so micro-breweries that have been born in the past three or four years, although several have also quickly died.

This has not simply been a continuation of my earlier search through Bavaria, chronicled in the Good Beer Guide to Munich & Bavaria, for the elusive perfect pint, although a good number of delicious beers have been discovered along the Czech way and are revealed in these pages. It has been more a journey of record to pinpoint the who, what, why, where, when and how of Czech brewing at the end of the twentieth century. The book reports that there is much still to celebrate in this most excellent of brewing nations, and some Czech brews other than the famous Pilsner Urquell and Budweiser Budvar are now trickling through to British, German and American bars and supermarkets. But for peripatetic imbibers interested in discovering the delights of the Czech brewhouse for themselves time is running out.

The years of negative Communist influence and neglect followed by the newer, harsher strains of a free-market boom or bust environment have seriously damaged – and will continue to undermine – the great Czech brewing tradition. The variety, quality, and plurality of the famous Czech brewing family is under threat as never before, and perhaps one quarter or even a third of their brew kettles will have stopped boiling and steaming by the year 2000. Now is the time to visit and drink deep while you can.

PRAGUE

No-one wants to wish back the Communist era, but Prague lost a certain innocent charm in the Velvet Revolution. Prior to the end of 1989, the capital of what was then Czechoslovakia was quiet, provincial, beautiful, safe and full of pubs which would have slotted effortlessly into a 1930s Hollywood movie. The streets of the historic centre were used as an open-air film set. Since 1989, Prague remains beautiful but has also become noisy, cosmopolitan, less safe, and full of refurbished pubs crowded with foreign tourists looking in vain for the set of a 1930s Hollywood movie.

Swapping the imperfections of Communism's state command economy for the imperfections of a market-led one has had its downs as well as its ups. The many hundreds of thousands of tourists who annually tramp through the city doubtless bring jobs and prosperity for many, but according to the Prague Post, Prague is now also the pickpocket capital of Europe. Wenceslas Square, where 500,000 Czechs persuaded the Politburo to pack up, is today watched over by knots of sullen, black-uniformed armed police to make the tourists feel more comfortable. The ubiquitous hamburger and pizza slice threaten the demise of the Czech sausage (klobasy). The pestering black market currency men – who used to give a square deal – have been replaced by legal money changers who charge commission and service fees; beggars abound; "non stop" neon service signs blink everywhere, offering everything from fast food kitchens to casinos that never close.

Restitution of property confiscated by the Communists plus entrepreneurial pluck not backed by sufficient capital or business acumen have seen many pubs, cafes and shops come and go. In 1994 alone more than 600 new licensed premises came into being. Many will fail.

Prague is a city in a state of flux, lucky for some, tough for many others. Basic services such as public transport remain super efficient and very cheap – a recipe, surely, to spare the so-called Golden City the traffic horrors being experienced by every city west of the now vanished Iron Curtain. But not at all; Prague is determined to have its share of shiny, bumper-to-bumper jams and fume-laden air.

If you can avoid it, don't visit the city in July and August. That's when the tourist tide is highest, when the Reserved signs are thickest in many city centre pubs as grim-faced waiters stand by for the coachloads of Germans, Americans, Italians and Japanese. And on Wenceslas Square you'll feel ancient and out of place if you are not 19 and wearing a mountainous backpack.

But for all that, Prague remains a wonderful city to visit – for the architecture, the excitement of a city re-awakening after the

Big Sleep, and the beer. Unlike most other major cities of central Europe, Prague emerged from the Second World War with only scratches, its rich array of Gothic, Renaissance, Baroque and Art Nouveau buildings intact.

In central Europe, only Munich, capital of neighbouring Bavaria, manages to evince an everyday beery feel the way that Prague still also does. Left to themselves, both cities would probably revolve happily around the same basic staples: beer, dumplings, pork and oompah music. But the world will not let them, especially not Prague which is inevitably homogenising to please the expanding tourist industry.

The urge to embrace "western" culture after the years of isolation has resulted in some dubious choices aside from McDonald's hamburgers and Tex Mex grill bars. Despite their own high-minded musical appreciation, from Smetana to Janacek, many Czechs are inexplicably having a love affair with American Country music. Don't be surprised if you stumble into a suburban Howdy-Pardner pub.

THE BEER SCENE

There is more beer choice in the capital today than in 1989, but the average glass of beer is weaker, more gassy, and dearer. The myth of something marvellous coming out of every beer tap is blindly promoted by the library of tourist guide books which have been written about Prague in the past five years, mostly by people who wouldn't know a Czech Budvar from an American Budweiser. One guide writer wrote about the "ales" of Pilsen. If they made similar gaffs about wine they would be garrotted.

Few pubs are owned by the brewers and until the industry settles down there is a supply free-for-all, which means that the beers listed for the pubs recommended in this book may change. Some pub owners are adventurous and go for unusual out-of-town brews, but for many more the choice will be determined by the discount or cash for tied contract deals of the biggest producers.

The two most famous Czech beers – Pilsner Urquell and Budvar – are now widely available in the capital. Before 1989 they were quite rare, especially Budvar, because the majority of production was sent abroad to earn hard currency. Today's cash-rich, out-of-town brewers such as Radegast and Krusovice are now everywhere in Prague.

Unwittingly, perhaps, the Communist era operated a supply system not unlike the medieval one imposed by monarchs who decreed that no beer could be "exported" more than one mile from its brewery. This led to the proliferation of brew-pubs in Prague. One street in the Old Town – Dlouha – had thirteen of them in the fourteenth century. The Communists were not so strict, but their supply-and-demand system was localised: for example Prague's Staropramen beer was never available in the Moravian city of Brno, and Starobrno beer never found its way into Prague.

Some once-traditional Czech drinking haunts, where blue-overalled workers mingled with dissident intellectuals – Vaclav Havel, for instance – are no more, or have been tarted up and turned into tourist traps, U Tomase being a glaring example. Consequently, prices in some central pubs, although still cheap for foreigners, have become prohibitive for the locals. And even in many of the cheaper back-street hostelries, drinkers have traded down to the weaker, lower-priced versions of their chosen tipple – the 10 degree instead of the 12 degree. It's called market forces. The price of a half litre of beer can range from under nine crowns (23 pence) in back street suburban pubs, to sixty crowns (£1.50) in trendy central bars.

Prague has five breweries; the biggest is Staropramen; the smallest and also the newest is Novomestsky, a brew-pub in the city centre (see Prague Pubs section). In between are Mestan, Branik, and U Fleku, which is also a brew-pub dating back to the fifteenth century, the last of a medieval line. Between them they produce about a dozen beers, from the easy-drinking pale 10 degree lagers to the thick, black 13 degree U Fleku brew.

Many pubs are really beer restaurants. In the central European tradition, you can call in just for a beer or three, or summon up a plate of roast pork and dumplings – often at any time of the day. Without a doubt, the quality and variety of food has improved enormously since the Velvet Revolution, but for vegetarians it remains patchy. Prague once boasted a vegetarian restaurant where half the dishes on the menu were meat. Perhaps not surprisingly it is now closed.

The traditional pub, especially in the central areas, is increasingly under threat not just from tourists but from the new entrepreneurs who have opened a mixture of the ubiquitous big city night bar and Vienna-style cafes, where you can expect to find coffee and cake or goulash and beer. Prior to the Second World War, cafes where people gathered for hours to talk or read or plot were a vibrant part of the Prague social scene. The cafes were the haunts of First Republic intellectuals like Einstein, Siefert and Kafka. The most famous of them, the Cafe Slavia, survived until 1991 when a US firm acquired the lease and closed it for renovations. Inexplicably, it was still closed at the time of writing – despite protests led by President Havel, who courted his wife there. The depth of feeling about the loss of the Slavia and what it represented was underlined by a group inspired by Havel who broke in and briefly re-opened it.

STAYING IN PRAGUE

The quietest and cheapest months to visit are November to April, excluding Christmas and Easter, but they often come with sub-zero temperatures and snow. May is relatively free of tourists but attracts music buffs attending the annual three-week Spring Festival which begins on the twelfth. June is tolerable and beats the student holidays. July, August and the first half of September are for the Eurorail ticket-holders and their rucksacks, and the blue-rinse coachloads. October is quieter.

At the top end of the scale you can stay at the Hotel Atrium, favoured by President Clinton, for around £135 a night; at the bottom end there are several camp sites —open April-October – where the tents can be hired. The cheapest deal is £3.50 per night per person for four sharing a wooden cabin.

In between lies moderation and mediocrity, ranging from fading Art Nouveau (the Europa on Wenceslas Square) to an ex-Communist jail where Vaclav Havel, a former dissident playwright, used to be a regular guest. One way of getting to know the locals and to learn or improve on a few Czech words is to stay with a family, renting a room. Several agencies strategically placed at the airport and main railway station act as go-betweens for a small fee, and they are the best, especially for those arriving at peak times without any booked lodgings (see below).

Below are some suggestions to suit most pockets. Unless otherwise stated, the prices given are average for a double room per night with breakfast. Tel-fax numbers are the local segment only. If you are ringing from outside the city but inside the country, add 02. From abroad, the Czech national code is 0042, + 2 for Prague.

Pariz

A CARINGLY renovated and very comfortable early twentieth century-style hotel with 100 rooms in the central district. £130. U Obecniho domu 1, Prague 1. Tel 2422-2151, fax 2422-5475.

Europa

AN ARCHITECTURAL oddball hotel of 100 rooms in Wencelas Square, five minutes' walk from the main railway station. Parts of the Europa are unspoilt, original turn of the century Art Nouveau; parts of it are Communist-era formica. Some rooms are cornily eighteenth century, others are furnished with MFI rejects. The ground floor cafe is a gem (see Pubs section). £65. Vaclavske namesti 25, Prague 1. Tel 2422-8117, fax 2422-4544.

Sax

ESPECIALLY FOR castle buffs, this tastefully modernised and well-serviced hotel is just around the corner from Prague's towering tourist attraction. There are only 25 rooms, so don't ring the day before. £60. Jansky vrsek 3, Prague 1. Tel 538-422, fax 538-498.

VZ Praha

IT USED to be an army R&R centre, but the present owners have made it more comfortable than it was for squaddies. Close to the Metro station I.P. Pavlova. £40. Sokolska 33, Prague 2. Tel 291-118, fax 2491-4441.

Pension Unitas

VACLAV HAVEL slept here – when it was a Communist detention centre. The interrogators have gone but it still has a utilitarian air. There are three and four-bedded rooms to bring costs down further. £30. Bartolomejska 9, Prague 1. Metro stop Staromestska. Tel 232-7700, fax 232-7709.

Intercamp Kotva

THIS IS the prettiest of three camp sites on the fringes of Prague, but well-connected by public transport. Kotva is beside the River Vltava at Branik in the south, near Branik Brewery. Its main attraction for budget-conscious travellers who are allergic to canvas are the four-bedded cabins which can be hired for about 600 crowns a night – that's £15. There are washing facilities for clothes as well as people and bikes for hire. Tram 3 and 17. U Ledaren 55, Prague 4. Tel 461-712, fax 466-110.

Ave (accommodation agency)

OFFICES AT the railway station (Hlavni nadrazi) are open 0600-2300 daily; at the airport there's a 24-hour service. Ave covers the lot, from basic rooms with the natives in the suburbs to top class hotels. Starting prices for a single room: 120 crowns (£3). Tel 2422-3521, fax 2422-3463.

Arriving

BY PLANE: Ruzyne Airport, which still has a slightly Third Worldish air about it, is eighteen kilometres (eleven miles) north of the city centre. A shuttle express bus service links the airport with the northern terminus of the Metro A line at Dejvicka and the CSA Airlines office at Revolucni street in the centre. It runs about every 30 minutes from 0700 until 1900 and costs 35 crowns (just under £1). Alternatively, the No. 119 city transport bus links the airport with Dejvicka Metro terminus every five minutes. Bus/Metro journeys to and from the centre cost about ten crowns, but take longer. Taxis cost between 300 and 400 crowns.

BY TRAIN: International trains from the west arrive at Hlavni Nadrazi station, which is in the city centre near Wenceslas Square and is linked to the Metro. An accommodation office (see above) is open until 2300. The Nadrazi Holesovice station, also linked to the Metro, is the arrival and departure point for eastern and northern connections.

BY BUS: International buses – including the almost daily service with London – and inter-city bus services arrive and depart at Florenc Station, which is near the main railway station and served by the Metro.

GETTING AROUND

Most of what you will want to see and sip is in the central districts. Prague 1 is made up of two old districts: the more historic Old Town (Stare Mesto) , which also includes the former ancient Jewish quarter (Josefov) and the "new town" (Nove Mesto). Both these districts are on the right of the River Vltava, just below the sharp river loop which stands out on all maps. The suburb of Vinohrady – once famous for its vineyards, but now packed with pubs – adjoins the "new town". Directly across the river on the left bank is what's known as the Lesser Town (Mala Strana) even though it is packed with imposing old buildings, leading up to the castle area (Hradcany). Below the Lesser Town skirting the river is Smichov, home of Staropramen Brewery. The Branik Brewery is in the south in the suburb of the same name, adjoining the river on the right-hand side.

Prague has a very cheap and efficient integrated bus, tram and underground (Metro) public transport system which reaches into every corner of the city and its outer suburbs. All journeys cost six crowns, whether it is three or thirty stops; there are no pay zones. You can transfer between Metro lines with the same ticket, but tickets are not transferable between the three services. The city authorities operate an honour system: you buy a ticket before you get on then punch it in one of the automatic time cancellation machines at Metro stations or on buses and trams. There are no conductors or guards, but there are plain-clothes inspectors who can demand to see your ticket. It's a 200 crown (£5) fine if caught without a ticket. If you plan to do a lot of travelling in a day or a weekend, it's worth buying rover tickets which allow unlimited interchangeable travel on all three services. A one day rover costs 60 crowns; two days 100 crowns. A month-long rover is amazingly only 320 crowns (£8).

METRO: there are three lines, identified by colour and letter: A (green), B (yellow) and C (red). The first line opened only in the mid 1970s and the last line came into operation in 1985. Extensions are planned. Trains run daily between 0500-2400.

TRAMS: more than 20 lines criss-cross the city and extend into the outer suburbs. Day services operate 0500-2400. Special night trams run from midnight. They are identified by white numbers at the blue stop signs. Normal ticket prices apply. The name underlined on the stop timetable is where you are waiting. Tram 91 is designed specifically for tourists and links up many of the main sights. It operates at weekends and a journey costs 10 crowns.

BUSES: do not operate much in the central areas. They mostly connect Metro stations with the outer suburbs.

PITFALLS

TAXI FRAUD: no-one seems to have a good word for Prague taxi drivers, who have a reputation for cheating foreigners. Legally they are obliged to operate a meter, but these are sometimes doctored. The best advice is to say where you are going and negotiate a price (see phrase guide at back). Officially, the base rate is supposed to be about 12 crowns per kilometre. Drivers can charge more for travelling in, say, a Mercedes, than an old Skoda.

THEFT: the flood of tourists has spawned an epidemic of petty crime. Prague has acquired the unwanted title of Pickpocket Capital of Europe. Simple precautions will spare you much anguish. The first rule is not to place all your valuables in one place. It may seem convenient to carry a single "secure" bag containing wallet, passport, camera and airline tickets, but that's exactly what thieves relish. It takes just one unguarded moment to lose everything, on a tram, in a pub, standing in the street. A friend of mine visiting Prague spent a whole day shuffling between the British Embassy and a non-English speaking police station after his "secure" shoulder bag was stolen; he had put it down beside him while sitting at a pub table. If you cannot leave valuables securely at your lodgings, disperse them in different pockets or bags. Never keep money, tickets, credit cards, traveller's cheques together unless they are in a secure, out-of-view body belt. Hip pockets are the most vulnerable, especially on a crowded Metro or tram where people are jostling. Not all gypsies are vagabonds, but some of the womenfolk are very light fingered. If you are male and a gypsy woman approaches you in Wenceslas Square, do not let her touch you otherwise you may discover later you have paid for nothing.

CHANGING MONEY: in Communist times dealing on the black market, in a doorway on Wenceslas Square, was 99 per cent safe, memorable fun, and the only way to get a decent exchange rate for the pound, mark or dollar. Today, it is unnecessary and potentially calamitous.

The official rate of exchange in banks is now approximately what it was on the black market before the Velvet Revolution, and as Czechs today can openly obtain foreign currency legally there is no need for a black market. However, tourists are still approached on the streets to change money. You might save on bank commission but you might also get lumbered with Slovakian crowns, Polish zlotys or, worse, worthless Czechoslovak crowns (the currency before the 1993 Czech-Slovak split). The safest and fairest exchange is at the major banks. Hotels give poorer rates, and the myriad "non-stop" currency kiosks are not there as ragged-trousered philanthropists: they charge commission and service.

CAR SECURITY: break-ins and outright theft are a growing problem in Prague, less so in the rest of the country. Anything detachable on the outside is also at risk. I had an aerial stolen.Whether you travel in your own vehicle or a hire car, find secure parking while in the capital. If your hotel has no facility, there are 24-hour guarded parks. It's worth paying for peace of mind. Two safe car parks are: Helios Parking Centrum, U divadla 77, Prague 1; PGS, Vinohradska 28, Prague 2. And don't think being a foreigner will excuse you from parking fines. The police take delight in the sport of clamping vehicles, especially German models. It costs up to 1,000 crowns (£25) to be unclamped. Some foreign car hire firms, especially in Germany and Austria, will not now permit their vehicles to be taken across the border into the Czech Republic. If you ignore this restriction, you risk being uninsured. A car in Prague is next to useless. Unless travelling in your own car, it is best to hire locally if you want to explore Bohemia at the end of your stay in Prague. International firms such as Avis and Hertz charge western rates; local firms are cheaper. Some worth trying are: Pragocar, tel 692-2875; Unix, tel 233-693; Rent A Car, tel 2422-9848.

GENERAL SAFETY: Prague is safer than most European capital cities. Muggings are relatively low and walking on the streets at night is generally not a problem. The Metro is also safe at night. But nowhere is perfect. Several areas have become a little sleazy and are perhaps best avoided late at night if you are alone. Or at least you should be aware. Dodgy locations include: around the Florenc bus station, the small park opposite the main railway station, and the back streets of the suburb of Zizkov, east of Vinohrady, where prostitutes ply and the bars are bottom basic.

In an Emergency

CHEMIST: look for the sign Lekarna. Most are open until 1800 Mon-Fri, but only until 1200 on Saturdays. Two which remain open 24 hours are: Lekarna, Na prikope 7, Prague 1 (bottom end of Wenceslas Square); Lekarna U andela, Stefanikova 6, Prague 5. It's between the Lesser Town and Smichov. Take Metro B (yellow line) to Andel station.

MEDICAL HELP: clinics where you can get immediate assistance from English-speaking staff are: Health Care Unlimited in the poliklinika, Revolucni 19 , Prague 1(24 hours, Metro B to namesti Republiky or Trams 5, 14, 26); Nemocnice na Homolce, Roentgenova 2 in the Motol suburb west of Smichov (all night service, Metro B to Andel station, then bus 167) and the First Medical Clinic of Prague, Vysehradska 35 (Mon-Fri until 1800 only. Metro B to Karlovo namesti). There may be a consultation charge.

EMBASSIES: British —Thunovska 14, Prague 1. Consulate section, for passport losses etc: tel 536-737. United States – Trziste 15, Prague 1, tel 536-641. Both embassies can be reached via the Metro to Malostranska station, or Tram 22.

POLICE: there's a station in each postal district. If you need to report a theft, you must go to the station in the district where the theft occurred. Few police speak English but they are obliged to supply translators to handle serious matters. Embassies do not deal with stolen property, only lost passports, a point you might have to emphasise to reluctant police. The Czech 999 is 158, but it's doubtful if the voice at the other end will speak English.

WHAT TO SEE

Even if you are only really here for the beer, a visit to Prague would be wasted without marvelling at the rich architectural treasures which justify the tag "Golden City". Few, if any, other European capitals can boast such a wealth of original architecture, stretching from early twentieth-century Art Nouveau right back to medieval Gothic.

Prague dates from the ninth century, when the first fortified castle was built. The settlement developed rapidly in the thirteenth century with the establishment of German-speaking immigrant communities. The immigrants were invited in for their commercial prowess by Wenceslas I (not the one of Christmas song fame), and developed the Old Town as a trading centre in the early 1200s. The "new" town was built only about 550 years ago. During the fourteenth century Prague became the largest European city after Paris.

The Old Town remains a jumble of narrow medieval streets which include traces of the former Jewish ghetto and relics of Bohemian grandeur, notably the fourteenth-century Tyn Church, the old town hall and astronomical clock. This area is also the home of the oldest university in central Europe, established in 1348, and the cavernous Art Nouveau Civic House, better known as Obecni Dum.

The Lesser Town, with a number of baroque gems, sits below Hradcany Castle; former residence of the kings of Bohemia and still dominating the city skyline, St. Vitus Cathedral, the national art gallery and a seemingly endless complex of lesser palaces and grand structures. The left and right banks of the Vltava are linked by the fourteenth century Charles Bridge, embellished with statues of saints, and now only open to pedestrians. It isn't all historic heritage, however. Like many of Britain's cities, Prague's suburbs possess some of the finest examples of 1960s and 1970s pre-cast concrete tower blocks.

OLD TOWN
(STARE MESTO)

THE LARGE old town square (Staromestske namesti) of imposing buildings which span many centuries is the focal point of the old town. It includes a town hall dating back to the eleventh century; a medieval astronomical clock (orloj) which has the sun revolving round the earth and puts on an hourly display of godly and ungodly figurines; the birthplace of early twentieth-century Czech writer Franz Kafka; a huge monument to the original Czech hero rebel, Jan Hus; and opposite the town hall at the start of the pedestrianised street Celetna the twin-towered fourteenth-century Gothic Tyn Church (Tynsky Chram) is well worth a peep. You can get an impressive view of the whole colourful setting from top of the town hall tower. To the east along Celetna you arrive at one of the finest pieces of Art Nouveau architecture in Prague, the Civic House (Obecni Dum). It's a mix of ornate exhibition halls, bars and restaurant all in a 1920s style. But to Czechs it's more than fine architecture; this is where the independent state of Czechoslovakia was formally declared in 1918 as the Austrian Hapsburg empire ended. At the time of writing the Civic House was temporarily closed for renovations.

If you leave the old town square along Maislova, westwards, you will reach the remains of the Jewish quarter (Josefov), which was a separate walled town within a town for almost five centuries until the mid-1800s. Highlights include the Old Jewish Cemetery, where because of ghetto space restrictions the Jewish communities over the centuries managed to bury their dead in nine layers. The oldest gravestone is dated 1439. The Jewish Museum, spread over five buildings in the Josefov district, holds a unique record of European Jewish life, ironically brought together for the wrong reasons during the Nazi occupation of Europe. The Museum's main base is at Jachymova 3.

NEW TOWN
(NOVE MESTO)

IT'S NOT so much a square, more an oblong, and despite its plainness, compared with the splendour around it, everyone wants to see Wenceslas Square (Vaclavske namesti). Not the castle, where kings and Nazi and Communist leaders presided, not even the Old Town Square with all its nationalist symbols, but Wenceslas Square, named after the ninth-century saint, the "Good King Wenceslas" of Christmas carol fame, is the place where the masses have gathered to protest or cheer or stand in insolent silence at some new invader. This is where the forces of the Third Reich paraded when Hitler annexed the country as a "protectorate"; this is where the outside world witnessed Warsaw Pact tanks snuffing out Alexander Dubcek's "socialism with a human face" – the ill-fated 1968 Prague Spring – and where student Jan Palach became a national hero in 1969 by burning himself to death in protest against continuing Communist oppression. This is where hundreds of thousands of Czechs defiantly rallied day after day in autumn 1989 until their unwanted Communist leaders got the message. Sad, then, that today Wenceslas Square should have been allowed to grow graceless with pimps, prostitutes, pickpockets and hamburger joints. Admirers of Art Nouveau should take tea – or a beer – in the ground floor cafe of the Hotel Europa.

CHARLES BRIDGE
(KARLUV MOST)

IT IS one of the oldest, most ornate and probably the most bent bridge in Europe. It dates from the mid-fourteenth century and is festooned with thirty bronze and stone statues; some of them are original, some are copies. The bridge, linking the two medieval Pragues, is named after Bohemian King Charles IV who commissioned its construction to replace one washed away by the swollen river. The present one is snake shaped because its builders used some of the earlier bridge's foundations alongside their own. The two didn't quite line up. Only pedestrians use the bridge now and it has a slightly medieval flavour by day with a rag-bag of trinket hawkers and buskers. Beware of pickpockets. The towers at both ends can be climbed for inspiring views. The night view from the middle of the bridge of the illuminated castle and cathedral is spectacular, and guaranteed to bring on a thirst for the nearby Betlemske Kaple (see Prague Pubs).

LESSER TOWN
(MALA STRANA)

THE NAME implies the place is insignificant, but it houses eight palaces and is dripping in ornate Baroque extravagance. The district was taken over and tarted up by the religious hierarchy of the mid-seventeenth century as booty at the end of the religious wars which Catholicism won. The rich residents later decamped en bloc to Vienna when that city was declared the capital of the Hapsburg empire and Prague's status was demoted. Ironic, then, that the Lesser Town was used as a backdrop representing eighteenth century Vienna during filming for the Mozart epic Amadeus. The Prague court abandoned the Lesser Town to a goggle-eyed poor. Some of them still live here in jaded houses-turned-tenement. But the bigger properties are now foreign embassies, and Prague's new rich are muscling in. Re-gentrification is under way – one American travel guide refers to "fragrant little tea rooms". Some old pubs have already fallen foul of this change, spruced up for tourists, up-graded into ritzy restaurants, or closed altogether. Two examples are U Tomase, once a monastery brewpub, and U dvou sluncu, former home of nineteenth-century working-class writer Jan Neruda and one-time watering hole of anti-Communist rockers. Wander through the winding streets of Baroque and imagine yourself a hovel owner from downstream faced with the prospect of moving into one of the abandoned properties. It must have been the seventeenth-century equivalent of winning the national lottery. Noteworthy are the Waldstein Gardens (valdstejnska zahrada) where outdoor summer orchestral concerts are held (next to U Tomase); and St. Nicholas's Church (Chram Svateho Mikulase) on Malostranske namesti, a masterpiece of opulent, some might say, grotesque, Baroque; the basic pub Vsebaracnicka rychta, at Trziste 22; and U Kocoura (see Prague Pubs). For Beatles nostalgists, there is a John Lennon "peace wall" on Velkeprevorske namesti. The wall, plastered with the ex-Beatle's picture and graffiti, became a popular symbol of youthful defiance of Communism in the 1980s, and even today the graffiti goes on.

Castle District
(Hradcany)

A WHOLE day, and then some more, could easily be consumed wandering through this fascinating aristocratic complex where people with a claim to rule first pitched camp in the ninth century. The castle has been re-built, expanded and re-designed almost as often as the change of ownership. The Hradcany is more than a castle: it's four palaces, the massive St. Vitus Cathedral, the national art gallery (in Sternbersky palac), and gardens with spectacular views across the ancient city. The cathedral (Chram svateho Vita) must have the longest builders' penalty clause in history – work started on it in 1344 but it wasn't formally finished and inaugurated until 1929. It stands in a large square within Prague Castle (Prazsky Hrad), which is a complex of buildings and battlements containing 700 rooms. The largest of the palaces, the Royal Palace (Kralovsky Palac), stands next to the Cathedral. If one structure in all this splendour can be singled out as the showpiece it is the palace's soccer pitch-sized gothic Vladislav Hall (Vladislavsky sal) where Bohemian kings were crowned.

If you do decide to roll up your sleeves and make a day of it in the Hradcany, there's a genuine pub at hand – U Cerneho vola (Black Ox – see Prague Pubs)

Nearby

There are approximately 1,800 castles in the Czech Republic and throughout this book reference is made to those which are in or close to detailed destinations, or near breweries. One which is not particularly near either, but which shouldn't be missed by castle connoisseurs, is Karlstejn. This 650-year-old stronghold, originally built as an impregnable vault for the crown jewels of the Holy Roman Empire, is 30 km (19 miles) from Prague. The easiest way to reach Karlstejn is by train; they run hourly from the station in Smichov, Smichovske nadrazi. The scenic journey takes about forty minutes, followed by a fifteen-minute walk to the castle from the station. But thirsts can be quenched at two pubs en route: the U Janu and the Koruna. The choice is from Velke Popovice and Pilsen. By car, take the D5 motorway for Pilsen and turn off at exit 10. Note that Karlstejn is closed on Mondays.

U Fleků - world-famous brew pub in Prague

PRAGUE PUBS

This guide to the best of Prague's pubs is organised in five geographical segments – North (including Holesovice which bulges into the river bend above Stare Mesto), Central (Stare Mesto and Nove Mesto – the so-called Old and New Towns east of the river), West (including the equally historic Mala Strana, or Lesser District, Hradcany, and Smichov), East and South. The pubs in each segment are organised alphabetically, on the second word where the name begins with "U" or "Na" or "V" .

NORTH

V CHALOUPKACH
(The Cottages)
V chaloupkach 40, Hloubetin, Prague 9
Corner with Sestajovicka
Trams 3, 8, 55 to Havana (two stops from Lehovec terminus)
🍺 *Staropramen pale 10*
🕐 *Mon-Fri 1500-2300; Sat-Sun 1100-2300*

Very friendly side-street pub-cum-restaurant where tourists are still sufficiently rare to warrant curiosity value. But they must be expecting you sooner rather than later: the extensive menu is already in English and German. The multi-roomed hostelry also has a chestnut tree-shaded garden, which on hot summer days makes a refreshing change from smoke-filled taprooms.The Chaloupkach is ideal for tram buffs who work up a thirst by riding to the end of the line. North-east of the old town centre

U CHCIPAKA
Sokolovska 142, Karlin, Prague 8
Metro B to Invalidovna, or trams 4, 24
🍺 *Nymburk pale 12 and dark 10*
🕐 *Mon-Fri 0900-2300; Sat-Sun 1100-2300*

A small corner pub beside the river industrial belt north of the old city centre. Its chief attraction is the rare beer from up-country Nymburk. The locals are politely shy, the food plain but decent enough and cheap.

U JAGUSKY
Na zertvach 28, Liben, Prague 8
Metro station Palmovka, trams 1, 3 5 8
🕐 *Staropramen pale 12, Mestan dark 11*
🍺 *Daily 1100-2300*

Budget-priced, down-to-earth factory workers' pub with a sense of humour and a written commitment to supping. The bar walls are decorated with paintings of witches and wizards, The accompanying Czech slogan says: "Give us this day our daily jug and forgive us our thirst". At 10 crowns a half litre – four jugs for £1 – visitors have no excuse for not joining in the commitment. On sunny summer days there's a small beer garden; in winter a snug off the main pub hall. U Jagusky is on the corner with Vacinovy. On the city map, it's on the right hand side of that big bend in the river.

U KARLA IV
(The Charles IV)
Srbova 1 (corner with Zenklova),
Liben, Prague 8
Trams 12, 14, 24 to U Krize stop
🍺 *Krusovice pale 10 and dark 12*
🕐 *Mon-Fri 1000-2200; Sat-Sun 1100-2300*

The lights dim every time a tram labours uphill en route to the Na Vlachovce pub (see separate entry), just as they did in inefficient Communist times. The locals don't seem to notice as they natter and play cards – or listen to the accordionist, thankfully only at weekends. This is a pleasant, traditional suburban corner local where the buzz of chatter doesn't pause when an obvious foreigner steps in. They've seen you all before.

NA STARE KOVARNE V BRANIKU
(The Old Branik Smithy)
Kamenicka 17, Holesovice, Prague 7
Metro C to Vltavska, or trams 25, 26 & 56 to Kamenicka
🍺 *Radegast pale 10 and 12 and dark 10*
🕐 *Mon-Sat 1130-0100; Sun 1130-2330*

One of Prague's new breed of pubs which manages to combine arty decor, a sparkling menu, and good cheap beer served as swiftly as the nonchalant nod at a waiter. The design includes old fashioned "snob" booths and a first-floor overhang if you want to gaze at the crowd below. Wall hangings include a 1930s motorbike and a portrait of Lenin. Fresh vegetables and kebabs feature on a menu it's best not to try to interpret – dishes have unfathomably silly names like Sarajevo Airport and

Zorro's Avenger. In late 1995, the Radegast 10 beer was less than 10 crowns – 25p.

NA VLACHOVCE
Zenklova 217, Liben, Prague 8.
Tel 664-10214
Trams 5, 12, 14, 24, 25, to stop Ke Stirce
Bus 200 from the end of Metro C
🍺 *Budvar 12, Regent 12*
🕐 *Daily 1000-2400; Accommodation*

A flagship Budvar pub with the novelty of a backyard full of giant wooden lagering tanks that have been converted into bed and breakfast accommodation. And this is no tacky post-Communist commercial enterprise – the casks were there providing fraternal lodgings before the Velvet Revolution. The main entrance is through a converted barrel, too. The pub has a Germanic air: pine wood furniture and live brass band music. Before the Iron Curtain collapsed the chief foreign visitors staying in the two-bed barrels were East Germans. In those days, Na Vlachovce was a rare Prague outlet for Budvar, now joined by its dark neighbour Black Regent from Trebon. Food here has a good reputation; a house speciality is roast pork – Vlachovoska basta. At weekends, a hall at the back beyond a small wine bar is a dance venue. A pianist occasionally serenades evening drinkers with Czech tunes. In addition to the thirty "camping" barrels out back, the pub also has less cramped guest rooms.

CENTRE

BETLEMSKE KAPLE
(The Bethlehem Chapel)
Betlemske namesti 2, Stare Mesto, Prague 1
Trams 6, 9, 18, 54 to Narodni trida, or Metro to Mustek
🍺 *Kozel pale 12*
🕐 *Daily 1000-2200*

A modest pub which immodestly takes its name from a religious shrine up the street. The cavernous chapel was an early preaching ground for fifteenth-century religious rebel Jan Hus, whose criticism of the catholic hierarchy helped spark off centuries of bloodletting across central Europe. The chapel fell into disrepair in the early nineteenth century and ironically it was only renovated after the Communists took power in Prague in 1948. Despite his religious fervour, they thought Hus was in the same revolutionary mould. A stroll round the shrine will work up an appetite for the pub's real claim to fame, apart from the beer: Betlemsky gulas – the house goulash.

BETLEMSKE NAMESTI
(Bethlehem Square)
Betlemske namesti 8, Stare Mesto, Prague 1
Trams 17, 54 to Narodni trida, or Metro to Mustek
🍺 *Louny pale 10, 12 and dark 10, 12*
🕐 *Daily 1000-0100*

Even in Prague there is only room for one chapel and one pub with the same name so this large hostelry, anxious to capitalise on the local Bethlehem theme, takes the name of the square in which

they all stand. The Kaple pub (see entry) gloats over its goulash; here they offer evening jazz with the beer.

BRANICKY SKLIPEK
Vodickova 26, Nove Mesto, Prague 1
Off Vaclavske namesti
🍺 *Branik pale 10, dark 12*
🕐 *Mon-Fri 0900-2300; Sat-Sun 1100-2300*

A cellar pub which has recently been refurbished and given more of a restaurant image. You wouldn't be too popular turning up here at lunchtime just for a beer. It has long associations with the nearby theatre, and playwright-president Vaclav Havel is an occasional customer – although possibly very occasional now that a partial smoking ban has been imposed. The president, like most of the rest of Prague, loves his fags.

U BUBENICKU
Myslikova, Prague 1
Metro B to Karlovo namesti. Trams 3, 9, 17, 21
🍺 *Herold pale 10, 12 and dark 13. Gambrinus 12*
🕐 *Mon-Fri 0900-2200; Sat-Sun 1100-2100*

Small, cheerful multi-roomed pub catering for locals and serving a big range of traditional dishes all day.

CERNY PIVOVAR
(The Black Brewery)
Karlovo namesti 15, Nove Mesto, Prague 2
Trams 4, 6, 14, 16 or metro B to Karlovo namesti

🍺 *Changing beer selection, including unfiltered Zvikov pale 10*
🕐 *Daily 0900-2300*

Half of this cavernous place is an old Communist-style stand-up buffet, a sort of Lyon's cafeteria of the 1950s without seats. There's a big range of hot and cold self- service snacks and meals at bargain basement prices, with beer naturally. This section opens at 9am for those who forgot to eat last night; the adjoining beer restaurant opens at 11am and comes with waiters and seats. Beers which have passed through: Pilsner Urquell, Purkmistr, Gambrinus, Krusovice, and the rare brew pub Zvikov, from south of Prague (see South Bohemia). The name recalls that there was a brew pub here until the end of the nineteenth century.

EDEN

U Slavie 1, Vrsovice, Prague 10
Trams 4, 7, 22, 24, 55, 57 to Slavia stop
🍺 *Bakalar pale 10*
🕐 *Daily 1000-2300*

The name is perhaps a little misleading. With room for 100 drinkers, the pub is bigger than the Little Eden (see separate entry) through the back streets near the Slavia soccer stadium, but Eden it isn't. It's also close to the beer "exhibition" pub – U Kloklone. Take in these three pubs, and a match, and you will be a little closer to Eden.

EUROPA

Vaclavske namesti 25, Nove Mesto, Prague 1
🍺 *Pilsner Urquell 12*
🕐 *Daily 0700-2400*

If you are going to stroll down the now tacky Wenceslas Square (Vaclavske namesti), you might as well enjoy the best piece of architecture on the street. The Europa Cafe adjoining the Hotel Europa entrance is a time-warped gem, complete with cummerbund-wrapped waiters and a musical trio who look as though they were involved in a plot to overthrow the Hapsburgs. A sign of the money-grabbing times is the 20 crowns now charged for admission when the musicians are playing, but 50p for a half an hour in a live museum is good value. Good for a late, slow service breakfast of ham and eggs. If you decide to stay in this central European Fawlty Towers, look out for the ancient lift operator who gave Adolf Hitler a ride while Bohemia was a Third Reich "protectorate".

U FLEKU

Kremencova 11, Nove Mesto, Prague 1
Metro B to Karlovo namesti, or Tram 3 to Mylikova
🍺 *Flekovsky dark 13*
🕐 *Daily 0900-2300*

U Fleku is Prague's version of Munich's bawdy Hofbrauhaus beer hall, and then some more. Not only does the place brew its own strong beer, deafen customers with a ten-piece brass band and put on a daily burlesque show, the new private owners charge everyone 15 crowns (40p) to enter. That may be nothing to western visitors but the money-grubbing ethos of the place – 40 crowns for a beer in smaller than average glass – puts it beyond the reach of many locals. Increasingly, it is filled with bus-loads of foreign tourists, predominantly German. Still, it's a must on any beery itinerary; the home brew is not available anywhere else, and the matching dark, cavernous rooms and shadowy courtyard do have a curious atmosphere, not least because the place has been there since 1499. U Fleku lays claim to being the oldest brew pub in the world. It's doubtful if there are any challengers out there, but you never know. Watch the waiters: they slyly try to dump a schnapps – to be paid for – on every new customer. If you are only there for the beer, tell 'em firmly: "Ne!" If you opt for the cabaret, it's another 100 crowns (£2.50).

U HAVRANA
(The Rook)
Halkova 6, Nove mesto, Prague 2
Metro to I.P. Pavlova
- *Pragovar and Kozel pale 10*
- *Open 24 hours weekdays; weekends 1800 Sat-0700 Sun (all night trams home from Lazarska)*

This never-say-die bar should be visited by all those stuffy, hand-ringing English licensing magistrates who agonise over an extra hour for some Darby and Joan golden wedding knees-up. The Czechs seem to cope without spawning anarchy, but then this is Bohemia. Why shouldn't insomniacs enjoy a beer and roast pork and dumplings at five in the morning? The Havrana is pleasant, clean and reasonably priced, although they charge a few crowns more for the beer between 10pm and 9am.

U HYNKU
Stupartska 6, Stare Mesto, Prague 1

- *Lobkowicz pale 10 & 12, dark 12, Lobkov Export, Kaiser Premium*
- *Daily 1100-0200*

After joining 10,000 other pairs of wide eyes, coo-ing at the Old Town Square (Staromestske namesti), and maybe climbing the 390 steps to the top of the Old Town Hall viewing tower, this is a welcome quiet, traditional watering hole. It's hidden from the pedestrianised, tourist-clogged street Celetna, just twenty paces away, by an empty-looking courtyard. Either the landlord isn't financially dependent on camera-whirring packs, or he's very myopic. Dark wood-panelled walls, spartan furniture and a wooden floor. But no sawdust. Sold Staropramen until late 1995.

JAMA
V jame 7, Stare Mesto, Prague 1
Metro to Narodni trida
- *Samson pale 12 and Regent dark 12*
- *Mon-Fri 1100-0100; Sat-Sun 1300-0100*

If you are only here for the beer, then here are two good species to spot. A rough translation of Jama can be "pit". This modern bar isn't that – the owners apparently prefer "hollow" – but it is a rather self-conscious Czech-American fusion. Still, you don't have to eat the Americanised food or mingle with the fresh-faced U.S. college kids or local trendies. You might even like looking at Elvis Presley wall prints. Prices reflect the origins of the pockets, but a jazz band drops in from time to time to add spice.

U KALICHA
(The Chalice)
Na bojisti 12, Nove Mesto, Prague 2
Metro C and Trams 4, 6 16 to I.P. Pavlova
🍺 *Pilsner Urquell 12, Purkmistr 12*
◑ *Daily 1100-2300*

The haunt of the Good Soldier Svejk (Schweik) – perhaps the most famous of fictional Czech characters – is no longer the way writer Jaroslav Hasek would remember it. Even in Communist times its fame was milked for the then limited tourist trade. This is the pub where Hasek, a true womanising, boozing Bohemian in the western sense of the word, picked up old soldiers stories of heroism and indolence. Out of that, Svejk was born. So don't be surprised to find fellow foreigners here aplenty, and Czechs dressed in Hapsburg army uniforms and walrus moustaches. The pub has been so over played, it no longer features in many "discerning" travel guides. Perhaps it will thus be able to regain some self-respect. For the time being, the neighbourhood evokes the flavour of times past.

U KRALE JIRIHO
(The King George)
Liliova 10, Stare Mesto, Prague 1
Metro A to Staromestska
🍺 *Platan pale 10, 11,12, and dark 10*
◑ *Daily 1400-2400*

A newish pub in an ancient, stone-arched cellar which in the evenings can get crowded with Prague's native bright young things. Rising market forces in Prague are forcing more drinkers underground where Czech entrepreneurs can afford the rent to set up business. This cellar is said to date from the thirteenth century and has been tastefully furbished in traditional Czech pub style. The city's resident expatriate bright young things congregate upstairs in the James Joyce, one of a rash of so-called Irish bars which have broken out across Europe and which no self-respecting real Irishman looking for the crack would go near. Why go to Prague to drink Guinness? The cellar is cheaper and more pleasant, once you've found it hidden off a yard.

KRUSOVICKA PIVNICE
Siroka 20, Stare Mesto, Prague 1
Metro A to Staromestska
🍺 *Krusovice pale and dark 10. Occasionally pale 12*
◑ *Daily 1100-0100*

A down-to-earth, one-roomed brick-floored pub, popular at lunchtime with locals who have nicknamed the place Brcalka because of the dominant dark green interior. The hook hanging on the wall behind the beer fonts rates a mention in one of Czech writer Bohumil Hrabal's books. Given the amount of time he seems to have spent in Prague's pubs, how did he find the time to write? This is not a place to go for a feast, but you can buy three beers for £1 and still get change.

LITTLE EDEN
Ruska 138, Vrsovice, Prague 10
Trams 4, 7, 22, 24, 55, 57 to Slavia stop
🍺 *Lobkowiczky pale 10, Staropramen pale 12*
◑ *Daily 1200-2300*

Another interesting out-of-town beer offering from a rich seam of friendly workers' pubs in Vrsovice suburb. Folk round here are discerning politically, too. This locality was the scene of some of the fiercest street resistance when Soviet-led Warsaw Pact tanks rolled into Prague in August 1968 to "liberate" the city from people who thought it was a reasonable idea to humanise Communism.

U MEDVIDKU
(The Little Bears)
Na Perstyne 5, Stare Mesto, Prague 1
Public transport to Narodni trida; near K-Mart department store
🍺 *Budvar 12 and Regent dark 12*
🕐 *Daily 1100-2300*

U medvidku has been a brewery, a music hall, a haunt of high-powered city officials, and a scene in one of Czech writer Jiri Marek's detective stories. Even President Vaclav Havel has fond memories of it. And, naturally, beer always figured in the equation. During the 1960s, 70s and 80s it was a rare source of Budvar beer in the capital when most of the production at Ceske Budejovice was exported. A typical beer hall atmosphere, with the added attraction of a summer inner courtyard. A Czech brass band, not unlike a Bavarian brass band, blasts away in one of the rooms. German tourists seem to like it. Two little bears are etched into the stone above the entrance.

U MILOSRDNYCH
(The Sisters of Mercy)
U Milosrdnych 12, Stare Mesto, Prague 1
Trams 5, 14, 26, 53 to Dlouha trida

🍺 *Gambrinus pale 10 , Pilsner Urquell 12, Krusovice dark 10. Sometimes Primus pale 10.*
🕐 *Daily 1000-2200*

If you're in the street you're in the pub, or vice versa, since they uninspiringly share the same name. The pub also shares the street with Bohemia's oldest religious monument, the thirteenth-century former St. Agnes Convent (Klaster sv. Anezky), which is now a state art gallery. U Milosrydnych (the pub) is a tastefully renovated three-roomed hostelry offering up a selection of beers and good food to a mix of locals and visitors. Round the corner on Dlouha street, records reveal that there were thirteen brew pubs in the fourteenth century. Must have been hell living there then. Today on Dlouha, there's the Roxy, with a mix of art, film, music, midnight tearoom and, naturally, a bar open to 4am.

NOVOMESTSKY PIVOVAR
(The New Town Brewery)
Vodickova 20, Nove Mesto, Prague 1
🍺 *Novomestsky pale unfiltered*
🕐 *Daily 1100-2300*

Prague's late twentieth-century brew pub is easily missed without a good city-centre street map. The entrance is poorly marked and via a shopping arcade. It's the most unlikely of places to brew beer, amid a warren of subterranean rooms linked by corridors with gaily painted wall murals. It's frequented by curious groups of Czech and foreign tourists not bothered about paying 20 crowns for a beer which tastes green and in need of more lagering. Despite the home-spun product, there's an accent on mediocre food, and the place is stuffy and sticky. Segments of the brewery – opened in 1994 – can be spotted through windows along the interlocking corridors. Strictly novelty value.

PASEKA
(The Clearing)
Ibsenova 1, Vinohrady, Prague 2
Metro to Namesti Miru. Trams 4, 16, 22, 51, 57 (pub in northern corner of square)
- *Gambrinus pale 10 and 12, Purkmistr dark 12*
- *Daily 1100-2230*

A pub peopled by Czech literary folk, many of whom are connected with an adjoining book firm. Given the keen interest these inky imbibers have in beer, it's not surprising that pub life is featured so much in Czech literature. Be careful, you might be lucky enough to stumble into one of their frequent publishing parties. They also occasionally have lively piano evenings with the ivories tickled well into the night. Namesti Miru is the heart of Vinohrady, a suburb of nineteenth-century apartment blocks built for a rising meritocracy and since the end of Communism again becoming fashionable among the new rich. The square houses the home of one of Prague's top orchestras. Paseka offers good Czech food at keen prices.

U PINKASU
Jungmannovo namesti 15, Nove Mesto, Prague 1
Metro to Mustek. Close to Wenceslas Square (Vaclavske namesti)
- *Pilsner Urquell 12, Purkmistr dark 12, Staropramen pale 10*
- *Daily 0900-2400*

Probably the best place in Prague to drink Pilsner Urquell, now joined by other beers which may change from time to time. White-coated waiters swarm over two floors, just as they have done since the mid-nineteenth century, carrying armfuls of brimming glasses. U Pinkasu is named after tailor Jakob Pinkas who was the first to bring Pilsner Urquell to Prague after a restrictive medieval ban on outside beer was lifted. This is an historic pub which seems to successfully manage the delicate act of catering for loyal local regulars and the passing tourist trade. Prices are not exorbitant, food is plain but wholesome and some of the rooms are reserved for drinking only.

PIVNI BAR EGGENBERG
Elisky Krasnohorske 14, Stare Mesto, Prague 1
Trams 17, 51, 54 to Pravicka faculta
- *Eggenberg pale 12*
- *Daily 1100-2300*

A small, crowded bar, popular with students who like to smoke like chimneys, and drink this rare beer from one of Europe's most unspoilt medieval brewing towns – Cesky Krumlov in south Bohemia. The newish Pivni is hiding behind the Hotel Intercontinental. Eggenberg beers are also sold in the more traditional U Houdku in Zizkov suburb (see East).

U PRAVDU
(The Truth)
Zitna 15, Prague 1
Near Karlovo namesti (Charles Square)
- *Radegast and Staropramen pale 10 and 12*
- *Mon-Fri 1000-2300; Sat-Sun 1100-2300*

For a place blessed with warm summers and such a thirst for beer, Prague is strangely short of pleasant beer gardens. The refurbished Pravdu has made some effort to provide a little outdoor drinking, if not far from the madding crowd then at least free of smelly traffic. A peaceful inner courtyard boasts two great chestnut trees, but if you arrive too late in the afternoon you will probably have to drink your beer in the smoky hall. U Pravdu's renovation gives it a Jekyll and Hyde character: to the left of the entrance is a nineteenth-century-style cafe with contemporary art hanging on the wall – the sort of place Einstein, Kafka and Siefert might have felt at home in; to the right – and at lower prices – is a beer hall in which the good soldier Schweik would definitely have dallied. Take your pick.

RADEGAST PIVNICE
Templova, Stare Mesto, Prague 1
Near namesti Republiky
- *Radegast pale 10 and 12*
- *Daily 1100-2400*

Not a very original name for an otherwise pleasant but ordinary beer hall, catering for locals and stray tourists. Swift beer service and a good selection of reasonably priced hot and cold food served all day.

U RADNICKYCH
Havelska 508, Prague 1
Between Metro Mustek and Staromestske namesti
- *Herold pale 10, 12, dark 13 and bottled wheat*
- *Daily 1100-2200*

New small pub offering an excellent out-of-town selection.

U VEJVODU
Jilska 4, Prague 1
In the Stare Mesto locality, corner with Vejvodovy
- *Staropramen pale 12*
- *Daily 1000-2300*

The wonder of U Vejvodu is that it is still there, looking every bit a genuine, weathered, centuries-old beer hall, and not face-lifted and made palatable for the homogenous tourist army which swarms outside and through the neighbouring medieval streets. Vejvoda was a town mayor who helped organise the defence of Prague from earlier marauding armies. Perhaps he's a lucky charm. The city authorities wanted to close and demolish U Vejvodu in 1908, but the Society of Friends of Old Prague intervened. The arched interior is a series of interlocking, ancient spartan rooms; in one you can eat basic Czech fodder, in another simply sup.

U ZLATEHO TYGRA
(The Golden Tiger)
Husova 11, Stare Mesto, Prague 1
Metro A to Staromestska
- *Pilsener Urquell 12*
- *Daily 1500-2300*

It may be touted as President Vaclav Havel's favourite boozer and qualify for a "Bill Clinton

Drank Here" (once) plaque but, mercifully, it remains a peoples' pub. They queue outside patiently before opening time, and five minutes after the doors are unlocked it is usually full – then you won't get in until a place becomes free; there's no standing. Artists, writers, workers, plotters and probably secret policemen have gathered here since the days of the Hapsburg empire. The mix may have changed but the loud, impenetrable, mostly male, chatter hasn't. Neither have the cellars, which are said to date back to the thirteenth-century, although parts of the building above are only eighteenth century. Treat this endangered central Prague species with respect. If Havel really loved the place that much, he would have taken Clinton somewhere else to save it from the unwelcome, gawping, flash-bulb tourists who followed.

NA ZVONARCE

Safarikova 1, Prague 2
Metro C to I.P. Pavlova
🍺 Pilsner Urquell 10 and 12, Radegast pale and dark 12
🕐 Daily 1000-2300

If it's summer and sunny and you seek a change from noisy, smoky beer halls, then head for the tree-lined terraces of Na Zvonarce where the locals dance to a band. It's a touch dated but, hell, this is central Europe not the King's Road. Na Zvonarce is part-pub, part-restaurant and the diners get the biggest beer choice. Good Czech dishes which include three types of knedliky (dumplings).

WEST

BUDVARKA

Wuchterlova 22 (near Vitezne namesti), Dejvice, Prague 6
Tram 26 to Vitezne namesti, or Metro to Hradcanska
🍺 Budvar 12, Regent dark 12
🕐 Daily 1000-2200

Within a couple of streets you can sample the beer from three of south Bohemia's most noted breweries – Ceske Budejovice's second-string Samson brewery beer is available at U knizete Vaclava (see separate entry). This pleasant but plain two-roomed pub with an outdoor terrace completes the southern flavour by offering carp (Kapr) on the menu.

U CERNEHO VOLA
(The Black Ox)

Loretanske namesti 1, Prague 1
Tram 22 to Pohorelec stop
🍺 Kozel pale and dark 12
🕐 Daily 1000-2100

This is just about the last real pub left in an increasingly gentrified and tourist-plagued locality. The pub has the air of one which has been part of the scene for centuries with leaded windows, beamed ceilings, long, dark-wood benches. But its beer taps were first turned on in 1962 – even before the "socialism with a human face" experiment in 1968. There must have been a nostalgic tippler among the party elite up at'palace. U Cerneho vola is a no-nonsense beer "hall", populated by local drinkers who banded together in the early 1990s to stop a private buy-out. They formed a co-operative to maintain it as a real pub and not a tourist attraction. So, tread carefully. Food is limited to traditional Czech beer snacks such as bramborak and pivni syr (beer cheese). Some of the pub's profits go to local charity.

U DVOU SLUNCU
(The Two Suns)
Trams 12, 18, 22 to Malostranske namesti
🍺 *Staropramen pale 12 and dark 12*
🕐 *Daily 1100-2400*

So many pubs in Prague's historic quarter have literary associations. Usually they feature in some writer's plot, but in this case it was the home of nineteenth-century Czech poet Jan Neruda, whose ex-soldier father ran a shop here. The street is named after him, but the significance of the Two Suns baffles the landlord, who will serve locals standing up in the taproom bar just inside the door but expects foreigners to sit at the tables. Good for him. Jan Neruda, beer mug in hand, looks on approvingly from the wall.

NA FARKANE
Na Farkane III 32, Radlice, Prague 5
Buses 137 and 508 from Smichov to Farkane
🍺 *Bernard pale 12 and Granat 11*
🕐 *Daily 1200-2400*

A big refurbished suburban workers' pub offering an interesting pair of out-of-town beers. There's a big lunchtime menu at very reasonable prices, and a pleasant garden for summer days.

U KNIZETE VACLAVA
(Prince Wenceslas)
V.P. Ckalova 14, Dejvice, Prague 6 (corner with Narodni obrany)
Metro A to Hradcanska
🍺 *Samson pale 12, dark 12*
🕐 *Daily 0900-2200*

If you've wandered up above the castle you must be getting thirsty. This small, three-roomed basic boozer has a refreshing brace of beers from Ceske Budejovice's other, less-famous brewery. You are doing well if you can get the 12-degree version, which is hard to obtain in south Bohemia.

U KOCOURA
(The Tom Cat)
Nerudova 2, Mala Strana, Prague 1
Metro A to Malostranska, or Trams 12, 18, 22, 57
🍺 *Pilsner Urquell 12, Purkmistr 12*
🕐 *Daily 1130-2400*

A cheerful, long, narrow pub of three rooms end to end, each one a step or two higher than the last. It's essentially a locals pub which adventurous individual tourists wander into. Some wander back out quickly when they discover there's only beer cheese or other cold snacks to eat. U Kocoura is one of those old Prague hostelries which features in several Czech literary works. Those nineteenth-century writers spent a lot of time in pubs. This one used to be a royal pharmacy, although the large black doors are more reminiscent of a guard house. Today it's a quiet pub by day, but becomes livelier in the evening. If you don't like country and western accordion music, avoid Saturdays.

Na nabrezi

Janackovo nabrezi 1, Smichov,
Prague 5
Trams 4, 7, 14, 52 to Zborovska
🍺 *Krusovice pale 12 and dark 10*
🌑 *Daily 1000-2300*

Trams trundle right by this
newish cafe-style pub close to
the Smichov end of the
Palackeho Most bridge across
the Vltava. Na nabrezi is in one
of the handsome nineteenth-
century, neo-Gothic terraces
which flank the river on both
sides heading south; it could
have been there for years, but
not according to the records.
Three things give it away: large
see-through plate glass windows,
carpets and incompetent
waiters. But if you are in the
vicinity genuflecting at the
nearby brewery, it's worth trying
the out-of-town beer. Don't
bother with the food, especially
not the bramoraky – they're
miniscule.

Samo jidelna pivnice

Na Petrinach 42, Veleslavin,
Prague 6.
Trams 1, 2, 18, 56 to stop Vetrnik
and walk forward
🍺 *Louny pale 10 and 12, and dark
10*
🌑 *Mon-Sat 0900-2200*

One of the very few places in
Prague serving this excellent dry
beer from the hop-growing
region of northern Bohemia. It's
worth the tram trip to avoid a
journey to the dreary and almost
pub-less town of Louny where
it's brewed. This is an average
suburban boozer, with
traditional Czech cooking and
outside seating in summer.

U stalete baby
(The Ancient Crone)

Na Kampe 15, Prague 1
Trams 12, 22, 57 to Hellichova
🍺 *Pilsner Urquell 12, Grambrinus
10, Purkmistr*
🌑 *Daily 1100-2300*

Ancient it is not. Although the
building has been there for a
century or two, the pub is post-
Velvet Revolution and underlines
how they come and go in
Prague's new market economy.
On the same street, on the left
river bank just south of Charles
Bridge (Karluv Most), beside a
narrow canal, one old pub is
now an expensive restaurant and
another is shuttered by an
interminable ownership
wrangle. The owners of U stalete
baby have filled the void nicely,
in every sense of that over-
worked word. Decor and
furniture provide a faded, lived-
in country look, rather like a
twee Whitbread refurbishment.
For the people of Prague it must
be a pleasant change to match
the three beers on tap. The
menu is refurbished country
fare. Try skvarky – pork
cracklings.

U svateho Tomase
(St. Thomas's)

Letenska 12, Prague 1
Metro A to Malostranska
🍺 *Krusovice, Ferdinand, Radegast
pale 10, Budvar 12, Ferdinand
dark 11 (range may vary)*
🌑 *Daily 1100-2400*

This is one of Prague's most
historic beer halls which,
despite the imaginative beer
range, has gone full tilt after the
tourist trade. But don't pity the
sullen waiters their burden of
babbling bus-loads of German
and American blue rinse; they

were like that in Communist times. The pub's name is all that remains of a strong dark beer brewed for centuries in the locality, originally by Augustinian monks. It was a favourite with visiting nobility at the castle up the hill. The brewery dried up in the 1960s when the neglect of a command economy geared up to the big breweries forced closure. Nowadays, the strains of Dvorak, Smetana or Janacek wafting in from the outdoor summer concerts in the adjoining gardens may be drowned out by ubiquitous canned pop music which some clown thinks enhances the pub's appeal. Despite that, the arched cellars retain some charm. Not so the prices: 35 crowns for a beer closes the door to many Czechs.

U STAROPRAMENU

Nadrazni 102, Smichov, Prague 5
Trams 12, 52 to stop Na Knizeci
(destination Hlubocepy). Metro B to Andel station

🍺 *Staropramen pale 10 and 12 and dark 12*

🕐 *Mon-Fri 1100-2200; Sat-Sun 1500-2200*

Just a block from the brewery , this small, no-nonsense pub is an excellent place to sample Staropramen pale and dark 12 together. If you are in a hurry, you can grab your samples at the stand-up bar beside the fonts just inside the door off the busy street. More leisurely customers can venture further in and find a corner in the nicotine-painted snug. Waiter service is snappy. Basic meat and dumpling dishes come fast and cheap.

U TRI KRALU
(The Three Kings)

Nerudova, Prague 1
Metro A to Malostranska, or Trams 12, 18, 22, 57

🍺 *Lobkowiczky pale 12 and dark 10*

🕐 *Daily 1100-2300*

Not so much a pub, more a tiny bar which it would be difficult to swing the cat in. But it's worth stopping at on the long climb up to the castle, both for a breather and a glass of these rarely seen in Prague beers from the unpronounceable town of Vysoky Chlumec east of Prague.

U VAHY
(The Weighbridge)

Nadrazni 88, Smichov, Prague 5
Trams 12, 52 to stop Na Knizeci (destination Hlubocepy)
Metro B to Andel station

🍺 *Staropramen and Gambrinus pale 10. Occasionally Purkmistr*

🕐 *Daily 0600-2200*

U vahy is once again the unofficial brewery tap of the adjoining Smichov Brewery, home of Staropramen. It was reputedly the brewery's first pub outlet when production began in the 1870s, but until recently it had been selling only out of-town beer. U Vahy is a cramped, bustling beer hall-like hostelry which serves the local factory shift workers of this industrial suburb for sixteen hours a day. Go here to sup, not sip; service is sharp.

VELKA HOSPODA NA BILE HORE
(The Great beer Hall on White Mountain)

Karlovarska 1, Repy, Prague 6

Trams 8, 22 to the western
terminus (Bila Hora)
🍺 *Pilsner Urquell 10 and 12*
🕐 *Daily 1000-2200*

There can't be many pubs
anywhere with a seven word
name – exotic reason enough
perhaps to justify taking the
tram to the end of the line. It's
not just that you can play
skittles, enjoy a sauna, have a
massage, sit in a solarium, or eat
an Argentinian steak. This pub
guards the site of one of the
most infamous battles in Czech
history. On 8 November 1620,
White Mountain, up behind the
rambling pub, saw the Bohemian
Protestant forces routed once
and for all by the Catholics. It
consolidated the German-
speaking Hapsburgs' empire and
crushed Czech independence.
The pub building dates from
1628. The foundation stone was
laid by Austrian emperor
Ferdinand II himself who
thought he was getting a
convent to guard the victory
memorial he had ordered. But
the Thirty Years' War – a spin-off
from Czech Protestantism – saw
off the nuns and by 1689 records
show that the building had
become the first Travel Lodge in
central Europe, housing a
brewery, cooperage, stables and
accommodating all-comers,
including passing armies.
Overnight guests have included
Marie Louise, Napoleon's second
wife, and Pope Pius XII. Today
there's a main beer hall (U
posledniho mece – The Last
Sword), and several different
dining rooms, notably Na bojisti
– The Battlefield. Such pubs
don't come in twos in Bohemia.
History buffs note: 1,600 English
troops turned up twenty-four
hours too late to help the Czech
army at White Mountain.

EAST

U BERGNERU

Slezska 134, Vinohrady, Prague 3
Metro A (destination Skalka) to
Flora station, or trams 11, 19, 26
🍺 *Kacov pale and dark 12, plus*
   unfiltered (kvasnicove) pale
🕐 *Daily 1100-2400*

This is a rare Prague outlet for a
rare Czech beer style:
kvasnicove, or unfiltered lager.
Some brewers insist there is no
demand for it, but local folk here
stroll down to this big street-
corner pub in their slippers with
jugs to be filled. It's to be hoped
that one of the big, cash-rich
operators like Radegast doesn't
muscle in and push out the
fledgling Kacov. The landlord's
good beer taste doesn't extend
to decor, however. Why would
someone living in a city as
beautiful as Prague choose to
festoon their walls with
photographs of New York?
Locals crowd the small stand-up
bar, diners wait more patiently
in the adjoining room. Good
cooked meals.

U HOUDKU

Borivojova 693, Zizkov, Prague 3
Metro A to Flora Station or trams
11, 19, 26, 58
🍺 *Eggenberg pale 10 and 12, and*
   dark 10
🕐 *Daily 1100-2100*

A walk along Borivojova street
will demonstrate perhaps better
than elsewhere what a thirsty lot
they are in Prague. There's a pub
about every fifty metres along
this winding way through the
worker's suburb. U Houdku is
distinguished not only for
personifying a breed of basic
Czech boozer which will
eventually die as the country

changes, but also for its lovingly-kept south Bohemian beer. Late afternoon and early evening are the times to catch this hostelry at its basic best: crowded, noisy with the day's gossip, smoky, and never an empty beer glass.

IBERO

Konevova 251, Zizkov, Prague 3
Trams 1, 9, 16, 58 to end of the line stop Spojovaci.

- Starobrno pale 10 and 12, dark Karamelove 10.
- Daily 1000-2200

The only known pub in Prague selling beer from the country's second largest city is an earthy neighbourhood watering hole in the capital's oldest workers' suburb. Worth the tram ride for the beer.

U KLOKONE

Tolsteho 8, Vrsovice, Prague 10
Trams 4, 22, 57 to Cechovo namesti

- Bernard, Budvar, Radegast, Staropramen pale 10, Gambrinus pale 12, and Mestan dark 11.
- Mon-Fri 0900-2300; Sat-Sun 1000-2300

By Prague standards, this pub is running a permanent beer exhibition. It's a policy which others might judge to be worth following given the brisk business at U klokone. Come early evening any day of the week and seats are scarce and customers spill out on to the street where the proprietor has smartly provided tables and chairs. Locals with a big thirst wedge themselves round the bar; perhaps that's why some brands run out some evenings, especially at weekends. Lack of

storage space is probably the main reason. The pub, named after an owner from the beginning of the century, has had a post-Communist face-lift of sorts, but the ubiquitous pale pine just looks sickly. The place is made more cheerful by the soccer memorabilia pinned on the walls. First division Slavia's ground is nearby. The cheap menu caters well for vegetarians, and for 40p you can have a plate of sweet pancakes (livanecky). Live "Country" music chokes the place on Tuesday and Thursday evenings. Visit nearby U Bergneru (see entry).

ZIZKOVSKA HOSPODA

Konevova 25, Zizkov, Prague 3
Buses 133.136, 140 to Tachovske namesti,
or walk from Metro station Florenc

- Mestan dark 10, Radegast 10 & 12
- Daily 1100-2300

New but simply fitted out with dark wood benches and simple decor, the Zizkovska has lifted drinking and eating horizons in a traditionally down-at-heel suburb. The beer choice is accompanied by not-so-common fish dishes such as crab and salmon. One dish is called Zizkov Joe in memory of Prague's equivalent of sharp-suited cockney spivs. Zizkov was their East End. The pub draws solid drinkers as well as those seeking good, cheap meals. Beer under 10 crowns is joined by a shot of Becherovka for 18 crowns (under 50p).

SOUTH

U BEZOUSKU

Kvetnova namesti 5, Pruhonice
Rooms available, tel (within Prague city area) 6775-0551
Metro C to Opatov station, then bus to Pruhonice (10 min)
- Brew pub producing an unfiltered pale 10 & 12, said to be on licence from Bernard Brewery
- Daily 1100-2300

Although outside the city limits, this family-owned enterprise is easily accessible by Prague transport and provides a richly varied excursion. Since the old U Bezousku pub was restituted to its former family owners it has expanded to include a brewery, a bakery and comfortable bed and breakfast accommodation. If that's not enough to lure you out of town, the village also boasts a castle, botanic gardens, and a twelfth-century church. The pub has several rooms, a stand-up taproom for thirsty souls who can't wait for waitresses, and a skittle alley. Hot meals are served for much of the day.

U KONVALINEK
(Lilies of the Valley)

Zabehlicka 73, Zabehlice, Prague 10
Trams 11 and 56 to Sporilov terminus
- Branik pale 10, dark 12
- Daily 1000-2130

There are several good reasons for taking the tram to the south-eastern edge of the city, apart from the tram ride itself: choice, a glimpse at rural life, and a glass of beer for 18 pence, 28 cents, or 35 pfennigs. Zabehlice still retains many of the trappings of an ancient Czech village, spoilt only by the former Communists

attempt to recreate a 1960s British high-rise housing estate on the doorstep. But this is no Salford; it's 100 per cent safer. From the tram terminus, you reach U Konvalinek via a pretty lake, the remains of a seventeenth-century castle and a twelfth-century church. It's a short walk, which should also take you past U Roziho, selling Primus and Purkmistr beers (see entry below). U konvalinek is a small, simple, friendly, slow-paced pub; smoke-stained but spotless and full of gnarled old locals. Beer costs 6.90 crowns and the well-proportioned half dozen daily hot dishes – roast pork, dumplings etc – give change for £1.

NADRAZNI PIVNICE
(Station Beerhouse)

Pikovicka 2, Branik, Prague 4
Trams 3, 16, 17, 21, 54 to Nadrazi Branik
- Branik pale 10
- Mon-Fri 0600-1900; Sat-Sun 0700-1900

If you arrive in Prague early morning, or you've been whooping it up all night and still fancy beer and dumplings for breakfast, catch a tram to this southern extremity for a bustling early opener on the railway station. But not on Sundays: the landlord has a lie-in then and doesn't open the pub doors until 7am. No sense of public duty. There's live music on Wednesday afternoon to liven up the jaded shift workers from the very close Branik Brewery. But it's last orders at 6.30pm so that the landlady can catch up on her beauty sleep.

U Roziho

Zabehlicka 113, Zabehlice, Prague 10

Trams 11 and 56 to Sporilov terminus

- *Primus pale 10, Purkmistr dark 10*
- *Daily 1000-2200*

A basic, triple-roomed pub with a small stand-up corner next to the dispense fonts. If you chance along when some of the sparkier younger regulars are in, they will try out their limited English by asking about the 1 British soccer club everyone (almost) is sick of, and invite you to play billiards. Good beer at basement prices. Go to U Konvalinek along the street to eat (see entry). Try also: U Vaclava, round the corner on Za navsi 8, selling Kozel pale 10.

U stareho pivovaru (The Old Brewery)

Branicka 53, Branik, Prague 4
Near the junction with Mezivrsi
Trams 3, 16, 17, 54 to Pristaviste

- *Gambrinus and Staropramen pale 10, Mestan dark 11 and sometimes Purkmistr 12*
- *Mon-Fri only 1100-2400*

This hostelry has been tastefully refurbished central European-style – carpet-free and dark wood panelling. It's essentially a locals' haunt, but the owners must be expecting customers from afar; the cooked-to-order menu is in English and German. The bramboraky (see food guide) are exceptional and make a great accompaniment to the Gambrinus. Staff and locals are friendly, still retaining that cheerful interest in foreign visitors. U stareho pivovaru is two tram stops from the Nadrazni pivnice southwards at Nadrazi Branik.

NATOČ MNĚ JEDNO NA STOJÁKA.

"A quick beer, please!"

BREWING TO DEATH

THIS BOOK started out as a beer lovers' celebration of one of Europe's oldest brewing nations, but it could turn into a wake. There is no corpse yet but the Czech brewing industry is now facing the biggest threat to its collective life, worse than the effects of Nazi occupation, worse than forty years of state ownership and the closure of breweries through neglect and centralised economic planning. In fact, despite those closures, Europe's last classic lager brewing culture was preserved during the Communist era, albeit unintentionally.

The word classic to describe Czech brewing techniques is used in the same sense that people in Britain and the U.S. and Australia now understand what is meant by "real ale" compared with a dead, fizzed-up, pasteurised version.

Today, the structure and character of Czech brewing is undergoing fundamental change because of the opposite of Communism – capitalism. It will result in the closure of many breweries in the near future – perhaps twenty-five or more by the year 2000. Rationalisation all too familiar to western economies, coupled with a growing foreign involvement, will dramatically concentrate the brewing industry, reduce consumer choice and ultimately lead to a Czech version of the "Big Six" – the six giant combines which controlled 70 per cent of the British beer market at the beginning of the 1970s before they then began eating one another to produce the Big Four, who today control 84 per cent of the British market.

This is the inevitable fate awaiting the Czech brewing industry – only it will happen much quicker – because of a Thatcher-like Prague government whose motto, on the evidence, was: "No half measures, no halfway house."

But does it matter? Does anyone really care? It should matter to those who care about beer quality and choice – and especially when more Czech beers are finding their way into foreign pubs, speciality beer shops and even supermarket shelves.

The few intrepid beer hunters who ventured into what was then still Czechoslovakia during the 1980s marvelled at the rich, smooth, thick foaming lager beers being produced there. They discovered that production methods had changed little since the late-nineteenth century when bottom fermentation techniques were being perfected. Only sources of power had been modernised in most but certainly not all breweries – gas or electricity instead of wood or coal. "Sophisticated" developments, such as closed fermentation and rapid maturation in conical tanks as high as four-storey houses, large scale production, de-oxidisation, pasteurisation and carbon dioxide injection into the finished beer, were unheard of.

These were alien western practices beyond the Iron Curtain.

But since 1990 Czech brewing practices have been changing dramatically. The brewing industry – or at least the industry's accountants and the marketing managers – will say for the better. Beer drinkers say differently. Unfortunately for them, consumer politics is at best in its infancy in the Czech Republic. *

Czech brewing companies are fond of telling visitors that the consumer is king, but no-one asked the people who keep the breweries in business whether they wanted their favourite beers changed. Far from being king, the consumer was virtually never considered when the country's newly privatised breweries embarked on modernisation in the early 1990s.

The breweries have embraced western hi-tech without much thought for its effects on the character and quality of Czech beer, and occasionally without fully realising what they were getting. One brewery bought a German brewhouse system but didn't have the computer technology to fully operate it.

The objective of much of this modernisation is not to brew better tasting beer, but to produce greater volumes and to provide more "stable" products with longer shelf life.

Until 1989, Czechoslovakia was probably the last country still producing mostly "real" lager. Traditionally, Czech beer – filtered but not unpasteurised – had been packaged in casks which breathed. The beer was delivered to the glass by air pressure, similar to the system used in Scotland. This gives the beer a smooth texture and the famous dense head which Czechs like to sniff and drink through. Serving draught beer was deemed an art and among Czech connoisseurs certain Prague pubs were noted for barmen who could always draw a dense-headed beer. There was pride at the font head.

"Modernisation" has brought pasteurisation, sealed kegs and CO_2 pressure dispense. Fizzing up Czech beer is a virtual re-run of the kegification which bloated British ale in the 1960s and early 1970s and led to the creation of the Campaign for Real Ale.

Today, more than 60 per cent of Czech domestic beer is pasteurised. Some of the blame for this lies not with brewers but with a new generation of retailers and their wholesale suppliers. Some brewers privately lament the kegification of their labours and they choose to drink an unsullied version in the brewery.

Because private property was proscribed before 1990, the breweries today own virtually no pubs and supply contracts are often not worth the paper they are written on, with retailers changing their supplier as often as their socks. While many basic traditional pubs have closed for various reasons – property ownership tussles, bankruptcy, changing consumer habits – thousands of western-style cafe bars and restaurants have opened, although some of them have just as quickly closed. During 1994 in Prague alone, more than 600 new licensed premises were created. Most of them want to sell beer – with the minimum of mess and skill and the maximum of shelf life. In the post-Communist scramble for markets, brewers have felt obliged to comply.

When Bass bought a stake in Prague Breweries in 1994 they quietly conducted a survey of drinkers in some of the capital's busiest pubs, and they found considerable discontent. Summat was up, said many seasoned tipplers, with the beer. Summat was indeed up: their favourite beers were being pasteurised and bloated with carbon dioxide – for the convenience of those wholesalers and retailers.

But Bass arrived in Prague armed with the wisdom of two decades of consumer relations experience. To their credit, Bass management advisers persuaded the Czech producers to stop the 100 per cent conversion of Prague's leading beer brand, Staropramen, into pasteurised keg form and to continue offering the traditional option to pubs.

Outside Prague, the fate of the country's two so-called brewing jewels – Pilsner Urquell and Budweiser Budvar – remains uncertain. Urquell is owned by a group of share funds and Czech banks and in 1995 obtained a £40 million loan through the World Bank both to finance further modernisation and expansion and to help deal with other loans. The new loan was in part secured via German banks. A moratorium on foreign share ownership of Pilsner Urquell expires in 1999. It is widely believed that a major foreign interest will then make a move, although Heineken denies it.

At the beginning of 1996, Budvar was the only big, profitable Czech brewery still in state ownership, primarily because of government concern about negative public reaction if a foreign predator got hold of it, i.e. the American Budweiser manufacturer Anheuser-Busch, which in the past four years has brought enormous pressure to bear on the Czech Republic in its attempt to buy an influential stake in the brewery (see Bud Battle chapter for the full story).

The long-term independence of both Urquell and Budvar, and thus the integrity of their famous brands, must be in doubt. Apart from Anheuser-Busch, Budvar has had forty-eight foreign suitors since 1990.

Until the beginning of the 1990s, Urquell traded on its time-honoured traditions. Just as a twenty year-old single malt whisky's appeal lies in its quirky production methods and limited availability, so the world's original golden Pilsner reached its peak of perfection in oak casks stacked in cold, dank cellars.

The privatised Urquell could have carved a lucrative market for itself on these principles of exclusivity. If enough people are happy to pay more for a well-aged single malt whisky than an immature blended variety, or for a special claret, or a champagne, then why not also for a classic, some might say unique, beer?

Those in charge at Urquell, or their wealthy financiers, chose to scrap all this god-given PR and instead plant a forest of hi-tech stainless steel tanks in a huge windowless warehouse and go for mass production. The new Urquell factory conservatively cost at least £50 million, which in Czech terms is akin to the depthless borrowing and debt on the English Channel tunnel project. But worse than this, the rest of the Czech brewing industry viewed Urquell as the market leader and many other breweries have blindly followed their questionable example. "Everybody wants to copy what they are doing in Pilsen", said one small brewer in Moravia. It is now not impossible to foresee a day when Pilsner Urquell might be brewed somewhere else in the world under licence. Something unique and special to the world of beer has been lost.

In the post-Communist era Czechs are drinking less beer. As one savage sage put it: "During those Stalinist times we drank a lot to forget." That's as may be, but two other important factors are changing Czech social habits. One, in a harsher free market economy everything costs more, and there is less left over after the basic bills are paid to spend on beer. Two, the choices to spend spare cash on have expanded enormously. This mirrors some of the causes of the beer drinking slump in most western countries – and the Czechs haven't yet embraced the healthy living ethos which will further diminish beer drinking.

These factors have led to a reduction in per capita beer consumption – 160 litres (281 pints) in 1995, compared with 170 litres (299 pints) in 1993 (these figures will seem high if compared with earlier per capita statistics which were for the larger Czechoslovakia and included the wine-drinking Slovaks). In addition, the country has swung from 12 degree (around 5 per cent alcohol) beer to thinner, weaker 10 degree versions of the same brands. Before 1989, about 70 per cent of beer drunk in the country was 12 degree. Today, that 70 per cent is now 10 degree. Even 10 degree versions of Budvar are produced. It's as though some enforced war-time rationing of ingredients had required the brewers to water their beer, but the reason is pure economics: Czechs are extremely price sensitive.

Despite all these harsh facts, all the country's breweries are expanding capacity in a desperate attempt to grab a bigger share of the domestic market. Admittedly more Czech beer is now being exported than before 1990, but nothing like the quantity to justify the industry's major expansions of 1992-96 – expansions which are set to continue despite their inevitable consequences for many breweries.

In 1991, brewing capacity in what is now the Czech Republic was 16.5 million hl (10 million barrels). In 1994 it was more than 18 million and by the end of 1995 it had risen to about 19 million hl (11.6 million barrels). More significantly, in the first five years of the 1990s the ten largest Czech breweries increased their share of the market from 43.5 per cent to just over 50 per cent.

Who is going to buy all this extra production? Not the Czechs, not the beer-saturated neighbouring Germans, and certainly not the neighbouring Poles and Slovaks whose recent swingeing protectionist import tariffs have already undermined old established markets for numerous Czech breweries.

This was Prague Breweries' (Prazske Pivovary) report on the Czech market situation in its 1994 annual report:

"Over capacity led to further increased competition across the country as national brands expanded their distribution into the territory of small regional brewers. It is surprising that despite this pressure and the obvious switch by consumers to the more popular brands, that no brewer has yet been forced to cease production."

The surprise was short-lived. Early in 1995 came the first victim. The Pilsner Urquell Corporation closed the 122 year-old Cheb brewery on the Bohemian-Bavarian border. "It did not make economic sense with another of our breweries so close (Karlovy Vary)", said a spokesman in Pilsen. Urquell may have lost its classic brewing methods, but it had now acquired classic economies-of-scale thinking. Cheb – called Eger by the Germans – had a brewing heritage reaching back to 1300. At the beginning of this century there were nine breweries in Cheb. Now there are none. Amen.

The chairman of Germany's largest brewing combine, Binding, which has bought a 51 per cent controlling share in the Krusovice brewery near Prague, spoke in 1995 of a "duel" taking place in the Czech beer market. "Obviously there will be breweries that succumb. It would be illogical if all were to succeed", said Mr Klaus Peter Ebrich, a former banker.

This duel increasingly involves foreign players who are moving in from their own beer-saturated domestic markets to seek new business. While economically strong countries such as Germany and the U.S. have managed mostly to retain indigenous beer industries, the financially weak Czech industry is both attractive and susceptible to foreign suitors. And there are few protectionist laws to deter. By early 1996, the Germans, the British, Austrians and the Americans had arrived, either as owners, influential shareholders or with attractive deals which also bring in foreign beer brands to be brewed by the Czechs under licence.

Bass's stated aim is to acquire 25 per cent of the Czech market – a goal shared by arch rival Pilsner Urquell Corporation. Bass's purchase of breweries in Ostrava (east Moravia) and Liberec (north Bohemia) in 1995, together with an influential 46 per cent stake in Prague Breweries and a higher option there after 1997, means the Burton-on-Trent giant is already more than half of the way (16 per cent) to its target. These buy-ins means that Bass has control of or a strong stake in three of the country's ten biggest selling beers and two of the biggest ten companies – six breweries in all.

Bass executive Mervyn Childs told the Prague Post in 1995 that there were too many breweries in the Czech Republic. "As a competitor, part of my job will be to eliminate them", he told the English language newspaper, predicting that as many as forty out of seventy-one old established breweries would go under in the next few years.

Austria's biggest brewing group, Brau AG, has bought a 51 per cent controlling interest in Starobrno, the major brewery of the Czech Republic's second city, Brno. Brau AG intends to brew its Zipfer brand in Brno. The Austrian firm has also reached a loan deal with the south Bohemian Lobkowicz Brewery in return for brewing the big Austrian brand Kaiser there. The smaller Austrian brewing company Zwettl has meanwhile bought the Jihlava Brewery, south-east of Prague.

The capital – and the country's biggest beer market – is now ringed by breweries under foreign control or influence. There has been a lot of nonsense talked by the Austrians about endeavouring to sell Czech-brewed Austrian brands within the Czech Republic at competitive prices, as though there was something supremely superior about Austrian beer. The fact is, they are brewing these Austrian brands with lower-priced ingredients and Third World labour.

In the beautiful Moravian baroque town of Olomouc the under-capacity brewery there which produces one of the country's tastiest dark lagers has contracted to produce that most noble of American lagers – the Texan Lone Star. It too must be destined for Prague, where about 30,000 young Americans said to be looking for the lost world of Ernest Hemingway's 1920s Paris have taken up cheap residence. It beggars belief that Czechs would want to drink stuff like that, but with enough market pressure and the right advertising they will.

Some might say all this represents greater diversity and better consumer choice, but ultimately it will mean the opposite. And some who read this critique will dismiss it as unrealistic consumerist idealism which denies "progress" and the laws of the market. But the free market free-for-all was foisted on an ill-prepared brewing industry which was given no chance to learn the basic skills of commercial survival after so many years of living within a Communist system where competition was an evil. For this, the government of Prime Minister Vaclav Klaus must take primary blame. Their rapid sale of sixty or more breweries was like allowing unwanted refugees to set sail in leaky boats in shark-infested waters. Only the buyers of the biggest or most prestigious breweries, such as Radegast or Pilsner Urquell and Gambrinus had a fair chance.

Foreign interlopers can hardly be blamed for taking

advantage of a once-in-a-lifetime opportunity. For some it has been the brewery sale of the century. All this makes nonsense and humbug of the Vaclav government's supposed hand-wringing indecision over Budvar. The survival of a nation's brewing heritage was always more important than one brewery, whatever the brand and its world prestige. The only guarantee for Budvar's future is to remain in public ownership. It would not be unique in the world. Just across the border in Munich, the world famous Hofbrau, custodian of Bock and Marzen styles, has been owned by the Bavarian state since the monarchy abdicated in 1918 and forfeited ownership. Budvar has been profitable for many years and would therefore not be a burden, as Hofbrau is to Bavarian taxpayers. And in present hands, Budvar retains a refreshing sense of purpose other than just profit. At the end of 1995, general manager Jiri Bocek told the Czech beer newspaper Pivni Kuryr: "We don't simply want to make an enormous quantity of beer at any price. We want to preserve the character of our beer. We don't want to race against breweries who produce more, because some breweries have already fallen to only valuing quantity."

The other so-called jewel in the Czech brewing crown, the Pilsner Urquell Corporation, meanwhile merrily skips down the road to damnation. The company announced at the beginning of 1996 its intention to offer some of its leading brands for brewing under licence abroad. Pilsner Urquell itself is excluded from this fate – for the time being. The company made clear it was prevented from selling its soul only because of a government restriction on the Urquell brand which runs until 2002.

Because of their limited brewing capacity, which poses no threat to the medium and large players, the country's smallest breweries are most likely to survive the market battles which are under way. Twenty or so of them have banded together to form a separate association to that of the bigger brewers. Led by Stanislav Bernard, a partner in the thrusting Bernard Brewery at Humpolec, this association has managed to obtain tax concessions for the smaller producers.

Market dominators simply seek to dominate, always providing for the lowest common denominator of taste. But eventually the consumer revolts. Why else have 500 micro-breweries been established in the past decade in the world's greatest consumer society, the United States? Is it because the likes of Anheuser-Busch, which controls nearly half of the U.S. beer market, were giving consumers real choice? Or is it because beer drinkers tired of what the Germans cynically call Fabrikbier – factory-made beer?

If they are to fully emulate the west, the Czechs still have some way to go. But the only real issue unresolved is just how much brewing diversity, choice and taste will be lost in the Czech Republic before consumer revulsion sets in – as it surely will one day. Then the Czechs can have their micro-brewery revolution too.

* Two beer consumer groups now exist in the Czech Republic. They are the Friends of Beer Party and the Brotherhood of the Hop. The latter is linked with a group of supporters in Britain called the Campaign to Protect the Czech Brewing Heritage, PO Box 2945, South Woodham Ferrers, Essex CM3 7AA. The UK group is not associated with CAMRA.

Olomouc Town Hall

SOUTH BOHEMIA

SOUTH BOHEMIA is one of the prettiest and least populated regions of central Europe: thickly forested rolling countryside dotted with castles and countless small lakes where carp is reared. Woodland carpets nearly one third of the region. Medieval villages and towns which have been in mothballs for decades are, since 1989, being dusted down and renovated to their former splendour. One of the most beautifully unspoilt medieval towns in Europe - Cesky Krumlov - nestles in a fold of the River Vlatava near the Austrian border. It was elevated to the United Nation's World Heritage List in 1992, one place behind Venice. And some of the country's most famous and popular beers are brewed in this region - Kozel, Regent, Purkmistr, Prior wheat and Budweiser Budvar.

South of Prague down to the Austrian border there are eighteen breweries today. Some of them are old-established, others are new micro breweries. Travelling south they are at: Velke Popovice, Vysoky Chlumec, Benesov, Kacov, Breznice, Zvikovske Podhradi (near Pisek), Tabor, Strakonice, Protivin, Domazlice, Cesky Krumlov, Ceske Budejovice, Trebon, Studena and, on the eastern fringes with the invisible Moravian border, Havlickuv Brod, Humpolec and Pelhrimov. Pilsen is covered in a separate chapter. Places listed below are in alphabetical order.

The history of brewing in this region is linked with the great medieval fiefdoms whose princes and barons dominated life. The most famous were the Rozmberks, or Rosenbergs, who before they backed the wrong side in the Thirty Years' War were fabulously wealthy, owning a string of castles and ornate breweries. The Schwarzenbergs, who followed, acquired much of the weakened Rosenberg property and became one of the biggest landowners in central Europe until 1945. They owned dozens of estate breweries. The oldest - and certainly the most handsome - brewery, Regent at Trebon, is from the original Rosenberg stable and dates from 1379. But the most famous brewery in the region, Budvar of Ceske Budejovice, has far less ancient and romantic origins: it dates only from the industrialisation of Czech brewing in the late nineteenth century and was a mere one hundred years old in 1995.

BENESOV

One of the biggest castles in the region - Konopiste - is closely associated with the long history of brewing in Benesov. The castle was built in the late 1200s and records of brewing there begin shortly afterwards. Various small breweries in the growing settlement came and went, but for about three hundred years until the late nineteenth century brewing was concentrated in Konopiste. The present brewery - now part of Pivovary Bohemia Praha (the five-brewery Bohemia Breweries Prague) - was built by the man whose assassination triggered the First World War and inadvertently gave the Czechs their national freedom. Archduke Franz Ferdinand, heir to the Hapsburg throne, acquired Konopiste in the 1890s and evidently had a liking for beer because he also bought the struggling Benesov town brewery, had it rebuilt and then closed the castle brewery. His injection of cash resulted in 40,000 hl (24,000 barrels) in the first year of operation. An assassin's bullet in Sarajevo in 1914 stymied more than just Ferdinand's brewing plans. His brewing philanthropy was belatedly honoured in 1989 when Benesov re-named several of its beers Ferdinand.

The castle houses one of Europe's biggest collections of arms – about 5,000 pieces. Its chief claim on history is being the place where the German and Austrian kaisers met – only one month before Franz Ferdinand's death – to seal a joint military pact in the event of a European war.

Konopiste and Benesov are 40 km (25 miles) south of Prague just off the E55. The castle is open daily between April and October.

Try a glass of Ferdinand at Zimni Stadion in the town centre (daily 1000-2100), or in the castle's pub-restaurant.

BREZNICE

Extraordinarily for such a beer-orientated land, this small and poor market town doesn't care much for its resident brewery and townsfolk mostly drink beers from elsewhere. Until late 1995, there wasn't a pub in Breznice which sold Herold brands (see Where To Drink

below). But despite being for many years a small, broken-down, cash-starved brewery in a rural town of similar circumstances, it has had some extraordinary luck. First it succeeded in staying alive during a Communist economic purge in the 1970s and a brewery in the larger nearby town of Pribram was closed instead. And when Breznice was finally shut in 1988 and ordered to be demolished, the Velvet Revolution intervened. Its survival and resurrection are due to the efforts of brewer Stanislav Janostik who successfully stalled the Communist authorities' plans to knock buildings down.

Perhaps all this helps to explain why the brewery, which was brought back from the dead in 1990, is one of the most cavalier and innovative in the country – and it doesn't have to cater for a deeply conservative local market. Breznice was the place where wheat beer brewing was re-introduced into Bohemia after a gap of about seventy years. And against trends elsewhere, brewer Janostik has also produced a strong, black beer. Sadly, though, this full-bodied, meaty brew is mostly exported to Germany, but it can be found now in Breznice, Pribram and Prague (see Where To Drink, below).

Breznice is little more than a sleepy market square and a few pubs. Ironically, the smartest building in town is the baroque castle which has been richly renovated and turned into a museum. And yet an unpleasant odour hangs over it. The last aristocratic owners supported the Nazis during the World War Two occupation of the country. Both brewery and castle are historically interlinked and records trace them both back to the beginning of the 1500s, although the present brewery buildings date from 1720. The former owners have been denied restitution rights because of the Nazi collaboration. Brewer Janostik probably has more personal pride in his piece of brewing estate than anyone else in Bohemia and is pleased to welcome serious visitors. Call well in advance. Fax 0042-306-982-546.

GETTING THERE

Breznice is 70 km (44 miles) south of Prague, near Pribram, and 56 km (35 miles) south-east of Pilsen. It is close to the dammed section of the River Vltava and the smart Zamek Castle at Orlik. Trains and buses run from Prague, and buses from Pilsen.

WHERE TO DRINK

Since late 1995 it is now possible to drink Herold beers in Breznice. See also Pribram below. In Prague, you'll find them at U Bubenicku and U Radnickych in the central Novo Mesto district (see Prague Pubs), and also try Comiva on Lipova 15, Prague 2. U Klokocnika on Na Veseli 702, Prague 4.

KARLUV TYN
Adjoining railway station
🍺 *Herold range*
☕ *Daily 0900-2100*
A new pub and the first for a long time to sell the local brewery's beers.

HOTEL SRP
(no accommodation)
Blatenka ulice, off main square

🍺 *Staropramen and Kozel pale 10. Bottled Kozel dark 10*
☕ *Daily 1000-2200*
An old pub which has been renovated unobtrusively. Big mix of locals who take advantage of the big cheap menu and beer at 6.60 crowns.

NEARBY

PRIBRAM
A former brewing town 21 km (13 miles) north of Breznice with several bars selling Herold 10, 12, and 13 (the dark) beers. They include Rosa, on Pribram VII, He-Be, Lhota 79, and Kamera, on Zdabor.

ROZMITAL POD TREMEINEM
Village west of Breznice where the Restaurace u Franka serves Herold beers including the wheat beer.

ORLIK
A gleaming white castle favoured by the Communist hierarchy for out-of-town meetings and relaxing weekends is now a big attraction on the edge of a large artificial lake, which is really a dammed section of the Valtava. Zamek Castle has been returned to its pre-Communist owners – the Schwarzenbergs – who have turned it into a commercial attraction. Boat rides and castle tours (daily 0900-1700, except Mon) and a pub in the grounds – the U Toyka (1000-2000, except Mon), selling Platan pale 11.

The U Curku in the village also serves Platan pale 11 and hires fishing tackle for the lake.

South of Orlik on the other side of the dam there is a new micro-brewery and another castle at Zvikovske Podhradi. The Pivovarsky dvur Labut (Swan

Brewery) complex has reasonably priced accommodation too. The house pub U Labutu is attached to the micro-brewery – in the former maltings cellars of an old brewery which closed in 1957. The Swan brews four beers, some unfiltered, plus seasonal specialities. One is based on a recipe handed down from the old brewery, which had historic links with Zvikov Castle. Try also the pub U Vanu, near the castle.

CESKE BUDEJOVICE

Ceske Budejovice, sometimes listed on maps by its German name Budweis, is the capital of south Bohemia. The town developed as part of the medieval salt trade route through central Europe and as long ago as the sixteenth century was noted across the region for its brewing. The big expansion in carp "farming" in that century was also a source of great prosperity. Until the creation of the first independent Czechoslovak Republic in 1918, the town was almost 50 per cent German-speaking. Today Budejovice sustains a variety of light industry linked to wood from the surrounding vast forests, but it is for beer that the town is known beyond the Czech borders, although train buffs may know that the world's first horse-powered railway was established here in 1828 and operated a service 90 km (56 miles) south to the Austrian city of Linz. The horses galloped until the 1870s when steam power took over.

There are two big breweries – Budweiser Budvar and the older Samson – producing a variety of beers, but it is really only the Budweiser Budvar brand which is famous abroad today (see Breweries section, and The Budweiser Battle). Ironically, perhaps, it was the ethnic German domination of commerce in the town which led to the creation of Budvar. The Czech population literally clubbed together to build their own brewery. It opened only in 1895 – despite the "centuries of tradition" hype surrounding Budweiser Budvar. There were other breweries in the town then and it was almost certainly one of those, or perhaps just the German name for the town – Budweis – which German-born Adolphus Busch borrowed to model his American Budweiser on.

Perhaps the most blatant public symbol of Anheuser-Busch's determination to subvert its Czech rival is its plush three-storey "St. Louis Center" in the heart of old Budejovice, where the PR blurb invites visitors to "enjoy some of the best coffee in town and catch up on some reading from a selection of English language newspapers, magazines and books". How very philanthropic. Drop by, why don't y'all?

Tours of the Budvar brewery take place Monday-Friday between 0900-1400. Book in advance through Monika Filasova. Fax from UK 0042-38-26170. Tel. within the country 038-770-5201. A tour with food and a beer costs £3.

GETTING THERE

Budejovice is 148 km (92 miles) from Prague and 137 km (86 miles) from Pilsen. Roads through Bohemia are meandering but generally quiet. Regular buses depart from Prague's Florenc Bus Station – be careful to choose an express service unless you want to tour the villages. Express trains Prague-Budejovice are sluggish. There are direct bus connections from Pilsen and Brno.

STAYING

Accommodation to suit all pockets has developed in recent years, from beds in private houses to rooms at the renovated historic Hotel Zvon in the old town square. Details on the Zvon, Adler and U Solne Brany are given in Where To Drink. Additional information from the town's Tourist Information Office at Namesti Premysla Otakara II, 2, tel 038-59480, fax 038-59291.

GETTING AROUND

Ceske Budejovice is a compact town, and most of the sights are within the medieval square mile, which is a short walk from both bus and train stations. Cars are barred or restricted in the centre. Budvar brewery is a mile or two north of the centre on Prazska; Samson a similar distance south on Lidicka. The No. 2 bus connects both.

WHAT TO SEE

Apart from a visit to Budvar Brewery (see above), Ceske Budejovice's other main attraction is its huge square, namesti Premysla Otakara II – one of the biggest in Europe – bordered by delightful renaissance and baroque-period houses and arcades which date from a fire in 1641 that destroyed much of the medieval wooden architecture. During the Communist era it was left intact but suffered from neglect which

is now being repaired. The square, named after the thirteenth-century Czech king who founded the town, is worth feasting the eyes on at any time, but nowadays it is tastefully illuminated at night. A statue of Samson – the biblical figure, not the local beer, alas – stands in the middle. The small centre is completely surrounded by a green belt of gardens and trees which replaced the huge walled fortifications demolished in the nineteenth century. The best view of the centre, and the forests and hills beyond the town on a clear day, is from the top of the Black Tower (Cerna Vez) attached to the cathedral in the north-west corner of the square.

WHERE TO DRINK

ADLER
Klostermannova 6. Tel 038-35603. Fax 038-32616.
10 minute walk from the historic centre
🍺 *Budvar 12. Prior wheat.*
☻ *Daily 1100-2400*
An excellent place to drink, eat and bed down in comfortable surroundings at modest prices. Twin rooms are about £20 per night with a good breakfast. The Adler (German for eagle) caters for nostalgic Germans and even Germanises its address to the original Klostermannstrasse. There was a sizeable German-speaking local population until the ethnic cleansing at the end of World War Two. The Adler is mid-way between Budvar Brewery and the old centre.

PIVNICE U SREJKA
On ulice Karla IV, which runs off the main square near Hotel Zvon

🍺 *Samson pale 10 & 12, dark 10. The pale 12 is occasionally sold in unfiltered form.*

🕐 *Daily 1100-2200*

Boisterous and grubby low-priced beer "hall" catering for serious drinkers. Small menu includes three preparations of carp. The MFI-style furniture and plain whitewashed walls smack of a quick post-Communist renovation, but at the time of writing there was talk of the pub changing hands again and facing an up-market refurbishment.

PIVNICE U ZLATEHO SOUDKU
(Golden Cask)
On Siroka, one block east of the main square.

🍺 *Samson pale and dark 10.*

🕐 *Daily 1000-2200*

A smaller, quieter and cosier Samson outlet in the city centre than the Karla IV. Cooked meals.

U TRI KOROUN
(Three Crowns)
🍺 *Budvar 12.*

🕐 *Mon-Sat 1000-2200*

Small, basic, street-corner beer restaurant which serves cheap and sturdy lunches to accompany the beer.

HOTEL ZVON
(The Bell)
Premysla Otakara II (main square). Tel 038-731-1383. Fax 038-731-1385

🍺 *Budvar 8, 11, 12.*

🕐 *Daily 1000-2300*

The 450 year-old Zvon, a drab and forlorn place before 1989, has been returned to its former glory, and even if you can't afford the room rate (£32 single, £47 double, without breakfast) you can enjoy the best view with a beer (in summer) under the arcades facing out over the

magnificent square. The hotel, once a coaching inn, has an up-market beer restaurant and also operates a much cheaper classic Czech stand-up buffet where poorer punters can sup Budvar's 8 and 11 beers, and nibble quality snacks.

MASNE KRAMY
(Meat Market)
Krajinska 13, off the main square

🍺 *Budvar 12*

🕐 *Daily 1000-2300*

It looks like a classic purpose-built beer hall: long and narrow with arcaded alcoves, noisy, smoky, busy and bustling morning, noon and night, waiters in black and white at your elbow with a fresh beer as you drain the old one. But it's been like that only since 1953. Before then for 390 years it was the town's meat market, with butchers' stalls laid out in each of the alcoves. The conversion was inspirational, and must rank as the Communist era's most popular decision in the town. Today, you can be in, served, and out again inside ten minutes, or lose ten hours in the hazy conviviality, as some customers seem to do, but no visit to Ceske Budejovice is complete without a Budvar in the Masne Kramy. Classic, cheap Bohemian pork and dumplings to accompany.

U SOLNE BRANY
Radnicni 11 (off the main square) Tel 038-54121. Fax 038-54120

🍺 *Pilsner Urquell*

🕐 *Daily 1100-2200*

Perhaps only in this beery town would the pride and joy on the bar of an elegant restaurant be the gleaming white porcelain beer font. This is a rare – so far – bridgehead by Pilsner Urquell in the home town of its big export rival. The Brany has eleven rooms.

U PODKOVY
Rudolfovska
🍺 *Budvar 10 and 12*
🕒 *Mon-Sat 1000-2200*

East of the old town centre, along the road to Trebon, this is one of the few surviving traditional pubs which have been selling Budvar almost continuously since the brewery opened in 1895. The pub – formerly called U Brabcu – belonged to the brewery before 1948.

BUDVAR RESTAURANT (brewery tap)
K. Svetle 2
🍺 *Budvar 11 and 12*
🕒 *Mon-Fri 0900-1800*

It would be difficult to drink Budvar fresher than here. The 150-seat beer restaurant is attached to the brewery. It's mainly used for brewery tour groups and doesn't have much pub charm, but the food is as good as the beer. Ask for the carp.

NEARBY

HLUBOKA CASTLE
8 km (5 miles) north of Ceske Budejovice via the E55. Frequent buses.

Of all the castles in this castle-studded land, this one is probably the most unusual. It's modelled on Windsor. Hluboka dates from the thirteenth century, but has gone through several incarnations at the whim of different wealthy owners. The present oh-so-English structure, with matching English parkland, results from a visit to England by members of the Schwarzenberg nobility in the early nineteenth century. Princess Eleonora Lichtenstein saw Queen Victoria's Berkshire pad and told hubby Jan Adolf II: "I must have one." And so it was – including Elizabethan and Jacobean interiors and leaded windows. In the village high street below the castle it is more typically Czech. Restaurace Obec (next to the church) serves Samson pale and dark 10. Daily 1100-2200.

CESKY KRUMLOV
Even the most casually interested surveyor of old buildings could surely not fail to be awestruck by the time-warped, medieval beauty of this small town built in a tight loop of the River Vlatava which flows down to Prague. To the modern eye, it's as though some witch had cast a Sleeping Beauty-like spell over the entire edifice. But the spell is now wearing off, and despite Krumlov's UNESCO world heritage status and the more tourists who "discover" it, the more it will wake up and change. The Communist planners managed to build a clutch of concrete, multi-storey blocks of flats on the outskirts but surprisingly – given the proximity of large-scale brewing in Ceske Budejovice – they left the ancient brewery intact as a functioning part of the living museum.

Cesky Krumlov is a monument to the aristocratic Rosenberg (Rozmberk) family who dominated this region for several centuries until a mixture of rare philanthropy and war debts forced them to sell up. Their biggest mistake was to back the wrong side in the mid-fifteenth-century religious wars between Catholics and anti-papal Hussites. Ironically, the new private owners of the town's brewery have chosen to name themselves after a lesser aristocratic family which followed – Eggenberg. But it is the Rosenberg's one-time armoury which the brewery now occupies; some of the brewery buildings are 430 years old and enjoy protected monument status. A good view of the brewery's layout is from Panorama Terasa (see Where To Drink, below). Today's brewery name was picked for purely commercial reasons – even though it is a German name, Eggenberg has more resonance for export markets and it is much easier to pronounce than the last pre-Communist era owner, Schwarzenberg. The brewery is at the centre of a revived annual folk festival – the Celebration of the Rose, linked to the Rosenberg dynasty – which is held on a weekend in mid-June.

Krumlov's tourist information office is at Zamek 57, tel-fax 0337-4605.

GETTING THERE

Buses and trains from Prague involve a change at Ceske Budejovice; allow several hours travelling time.

STAYING

Krumlov is by far the cheapest and prettiest place in the region to stay for several nights. It's possible to rent a double room in the heart of the old town overlooking the castle and river for £12.50 a day, with hearty breakfast. The street called Parkan with a line of cottages edging the river whose owners have gone into the bed and breakfast business offers the best

deals. Mrs Stindlova's Pension U Vlatava has excellent modernised en suite rooms at No. 107 for about 500 crowns. Tel 0337-4396. Similar is U Marii at No. 104. Tel 0337-5228. Booking in advance for these gems is advisable. The pub Hospoda na Louzi (see Where To Drink below) has modern rooms at about 900 crowns. More up market is the Straninger (see below), and the Krumlov, an old but cosy hotel on the main square (namesti Svornosti 14, tel 0337-2255, fax 0337-3498. The biggest problem if you are travelling by car is parking. The medieval streets are too narrow for modern traffic and quite rightly severe restrictions apply, but if you are an over-night visitor you can obtain a free parking permit – provided there's room.

WHAT TO SEE

The single most striking feature of Krumlov is the castle, the biggest in Bohemia after Prague. It literally hangs over the old town, perched on the edge of a rocky cliff with a sheer drop of a hundred feet. Parts date back to the 1200s, but the bulk of the structure is sixteenth-century renaissance. Its three hundred rooms are stuffed with art treasures. The castle's ornate theatre is one of Europe's baroque wonders. An amazing multiple-arched bridge links the sprawling castle across the craggy cliff. Views from the towering and gaily-frescoed castle keep – which vaguely resembles a mosque's minaret – are spectacular. The town was originally two – Krumlov and Latran – where today's brewery stands. Silver mining in the surrounding hills was the original source of wealth and trading in the area and Cesky Krumlov's one-time prosperity can be gauged by the ornate town hall (Radnice) in the main square. But brewing was always an important part of the town's life, and the original municipal brewhouse still stands between the street Siroka and the river, facing away from the castle. For train buffs, the town museum at Horni 152 houses a model of the horse-drawn railway which linked Ceske Budejovice, via Krumlov, with Linz (see Budejovice notes).

WHERE TO DRINK

RESTAURACE VIDEN
(The Vienna)
Latran 3, old town
🍺 *Eggenberg pale 12*
🕐 *Daily 1000-2200*
A quiet, basic, unrenovated pub near the brewery on the cobbled main street of the old town.

U KALICHA
Latran 13, old town
🍺 *Budvar 12, Regent pale 12.*
🕐 *Daily 1000-2300*
Two excellent beers in an unspoilt old town pub with a terrace overlooking the river. Cooked meals for £1. Look out for carp on the menu.

HOSPODA NA LOUZI
(The Puddle)
Kajovska 66, old town
Tel-fax 0337-5495
🍺 *Eggenberg pale 12, dark 10*
🕐 *Daily 1100-2200 (sometimes closes earlier if quiet)*
Tiny pub which slips back into the early twentieth century with its smoky brown panelling, rickety furniture and sundry bric-a-brac. But the landlord

confessed, over a mug of beer, that he runs a 1990s fake. Still, it's pleasant enough and attracts a mix of locals and tourists. And there's nothing phoney about the menu, concentrating on traditional snacks and dishes which go well with beer: Utopenec (Drowned Men – thick spicy-sour sausage), Bramborak (spicy potato cakes), carp (which goes well with the dark Eggenberg). There are reasonably priced rooms at the back if The Puddle gets too deep.

STRANINGER
Siroka 49
Tel-fax 0337-5104
🍺 *Samson pale 12*
🕐 *Daily 1000-2200*
A quiet pub which also has rooms. Drinking spills on to pavement tables in summer on the pedestrianised street.

PANORAMA TERASA
Kaplicka
🍺 *Budvar 12*
The best view with a drink in town: the terrace not only overlooks much of the old town, it provides a bird's-eye look into Eggenberg Brewery across the Vlatava River. On the opposite side of the street is the Restaurant Asia, perhaps the only curry house in Europe which also offers bed and breakfast.

PIVNICE EGGENBERG
Na novem meste, off Latran
🍺 *Eggenberg pale 10, 12, and 10 dark. Bavarian Arco bottled wheat beer*
🕐 *Main hall Mon-Sat 1000-2200. Side tap room: daily 1000-2200.*
Eggenberg is one of the few Czech breweries to date with a genuine tap. This one is two: a cavernous, high-ceilinged,

monastery-like hall where the clatter of knives and forks echoes eerily and pretty waitresses bustle, and a grubby side bar where serious drinking townsfolk gather to take advantage of beer at 9 crowns (23 pence) a half litre.

NEARBY

South-west of Krumlov, where the borders of Germany, Austria and the Czech Republic meet, is the huge Lipenska, a 19 km (12 mile) dam through which the Vltava flows. For those who yearn for solitude, this is the place. There's Platan beer at Pivnice Lipenska in Cerna. Rozmberk Castle, the twelfth-century stronghold of the Rozmberks guarding the Bohemian border with Austria, is 25 km (15 miles) south of Krumlov in the town bearing the family's name. It's open to the public, who are invited to try to spot the White Lady, a ghost reputed to have thwarted attempts by the Nazis to hoist the swastika flag over the ramparts during World War Two. The Gestapo held an enquiry into the activities of the White Lady, who haunted people who tried to climb the castle tower to raise the flag. The result was that the swastika didn't flutter over Rozmberk. Thirsts can be dealt with at the Ratolest with Eggenberg beer.

DOMAZLICE

Domazlicians lay claim to being the biggest beer drinkers in the Czech Republic. The brewery reckons they annually consume more than 200 litres (350 pints) per head of population, compared with a national average of around 160 litres. In 1994 the figures were 204 to 161. The town also claims to be home to Bohemia's oldest brewery, which allegedly dates from 1341. A more genuine-looking claimant is Regent, at Trebon. Perhaps the drinking phenomenon was linked to the town's plight between 1945 and 1989. Deep in the forested border region, this dilapidated town with a rich history was left to slumber during the 44-year East-West Cold War which sealed the frontier with Germany and closed off its natural trading links with the neighbouring Bavarians. But with the rusting away of the Iron Curtain, Domazlice has sprung back to life – and nothing more so than the town's brewery which is now part of the privatised Pilsner Urquell Breweries group.

The country's best known and most widely available dark beer – Purkmistr – is brewed here, as well as the excellent unfiltered wheat beer Prior. It's not surprising that Domazlice brews wheat beer; it's popular with border Bavarians who flock over at weekends to take advantage of much cheaper goods and services. Some come for a haircut and a beer. Signs in German abound, and social-cultural links are growing – such as cross-border soccer matches. Bavarians still call Domazlice by its old German name: Taus.

Domazlicians have been brewing beer since this border region was Chodian rather than Czech. The Chods were a distinct tribe who retained a level of independence until the fifteenth century when, like others in that war-torn time, they backed the wrong side in the religious conflicts and were put down in a rebellion which backfired. But some of their distinctive traditions and folksy images have endured – not least the habit of bagpipe playing (see also Strakonice). No-one has yet spotted a haggis in the surrounding forests. The Chods' cultural diversity is now celebrated with an annual festival in August.

Domazlice's tourist office is reachable on fax; 0042-189-2713

GETTING THERE

Trains and buses – make sure its an express – link Domazlice with Pilsen (57 km, 36 miles) and Prague (148 km, 92 miles) and Ceske Budejovice (137 km, 86 miles). Avoid the train between Domazlice and Budejovice, unless you have time for a slow, meandering scenic journey and plenty of refreshments with you. The Pilsen-Domazlice road (route 26) is narrow and increasingly clogged with cross-border commercial traffic.

STAYING

Reasonably-priced bed and breakfast accommodation approved by Cedok includes: Pension Na Varinecku, tel. 0189-8338; Pension Viola, tel 0189-2435; Pension Psohlavec, tel 0189-2226, fax 5052. Domazlice's tourist office is reachable on fax 0042-189-2713

WHAT TO SEE

As with most Bohemian towns, the focal point of Domazlice is the main square, which here is an exceptionally elongated, traditional oblong shape, flanked by attractive arcaded houses and shops in renaissance and baroque style. Examples of the Chod culture can be seen in

Chodsky Hrad (Chod Castle), on Chodske namesti off the main square. The castle tower is a guiding beacon. A few miles west of Domazlice is Babylon, a curious Communist-era, Butlin's-like holiday camp in the forest. Good for a cool swim in summer. Bavaria, and in particular Furth im Wald with three breweries, is only eight miles west of Domazlice. Between the two is Bohemia's highest peak, the 3409-foot Cerchov. In this richly-forested landscape, it's hard to imagine you are on a level with the peaks of Britain's highest mountains, the barren, windswept Grampians.

WHERE TO DRINK

All four pubs listed are in the town centre

U CERTA
Off the main square
- Gambrinus pale 10 and 12, Purkmistr 10, Prior wheat
- Daily 1000-2200

Popular with locals who enjoy varietal styles of beer. Good atmosphere and food.

KAVKAZ
Hajkova 479
- Gambrinus 10
- Mon-Thur 1000-2200; Fri-Sun 1000-2300

A traditional, if spartan, beer restaurant with typical Bohemian cooked fare.

HUBERTUS
Jiraskova 48.
- Radni 10, Pilsner Urquell 12, Prior wheat
- Mon-Thur 1400-2200; Fri-Sat 1700-2300; closed Sunday.

A small after-work bar behind the castle, off Chodska.

STIKA
28 rijna 85

🍺 *Radni 10, Gambrinus 10,
    Purkmistr 12*

🕐 *Mon-Fri 1400-2000; Sat 1700-
    2400; Sun 1600-2300*

An after-work session haunt and busy watering hole on weekend evenings.

PROTIVIN

A small town with a 500 year-old brewing tradition, Protivin also boasts a seventeenth-century castle – yet another former piece of the Schwarzenberg real estate. It was this powerful family which built the present brewery, set in parkland planted with plane (platan) trees from which the brewery's beers take their name. Remains of the fortified town walls can be seen fringing the large, open town square.

WHERE TO DRINK

BLANICE
Main town square
Tel 0362-92568

🍺 *Platan pale 11, Budvar 10 and
    12, Pilsner Urquell*

🕐 *Mon-Sat 1000-2200; Sun 1000-
    2000*

A plain, friendly town-square inn offering a good range of beers, cheap food and modest-priced bed and breakfast.

HOSPODA SV. VACLAVA
Opposite the brewery entrance

🍺 *Platan 10 and 12 pale.*

🕐 *Daily 0900-2100*

This is the nearest thing to a Platan Brewery tap, on the street close to the long, elegant driveway to the brewery which is set in park-like grounds. A basic boozer that fills with brewery workers and other thirsty townsfolk late afternoon on weekdays. Eat at the Blanice.

NEARBY

The town of Pisek on the banks of the River Otava boasts the oldest stone bridge (early 1200s) in Bohemia, older even than the famous Charles Bridge (Karlovy Most) in Prague. The town is named after gold-bearing sand which was discovered on the river banks in the middle ages. The U Tri Koroun (daily 1000-2200) offers Platan beers and beds.

STRAKONICE

Not only does this bustling small, but industrialised town have a brewery (see Breweries chapter) and a castle, it is the venue of a regular International Bagpipe Festival. The event is held in the courtyard of the fifteenth-century castle in the September of even-numbered years. A museum in the castle offers evidence that bagpipes are not the exclusive preserve of Scotsmen (see also Domazlice). One of the town's small industries is bagpipe making, which may have more of a future than brewing. In early 1996, the small nineteenth-century brewery was still state owned. Strakonice is also noted for motorbike manufacture.

U PAPEZE
Velke namesti, town centre

🍺 *Gambrinus, Budvar pale 12,
    Pilsner Urquell, Prior wheat*

🕐 *Daily 1100-2300*

Renovated beer restaurant with crisp white tablecloths and pink decor. A big menu at moderate prices. In the basement there's a more boisterous bar, open 1500-0300.

U ZBOROVA

Turn right into side street at bottom end of Velke namesti,
just before dual carriageway and the brewery opposite

🍺 *Nektar pale and dark 10, Dudak pale 12, Budvar 12*

🕐 *Daily 0900-2200*

This is a lively traditional pub, sympathetically modernised, popular with brewery workers from across the way. Solid, budget meals.

TABOR

Tabor is another new micro-brewery town. It's adjacent to the main square, Zizkove Namesti, and produces two pale brews and a dark lager called Taborsky kalich (Chalice of Tabor). Try also U Slavie in the hotel of the same name.

Tabor's medieval centre on a confluence of rivers is a beautiful reminder of its past, and of the emotional place it holds in Czech history. It's named after the biblical Mount Tabor and was founded in 1420 by the rebel Jan Zizka. The town became a stronghold of the Hussites, named after the catholic reformer Jan Hus, whose death at the stake in 1415 for alleged heresy sparked off years of religious wars in central Europe. Zizka was the Hussites' military leader.

TREBON

The twin red-brick chimneys of Bohemia's oldest (1379) and probably most handsome brewery, Pivovar Regent, stand like sentinels over this pretty town of renaissance and baroque, the "capital" of the region's carp fishing. Regent's buildings were originally the town's arsenal; the brewery was transferred into them in the late seventeenth century when they were remodelled to give them their attractive baroque facade. Like most things in the region, Regent was originally founded and owned by the Rosenberg/Rozmberk family, and eventually ended up in the ownership of the even more powerful Schwarzenbergs, until 1945. Trebon is now trying to revive its other pre-World War Two claim to fame: health spa. The surrounding peat bogs are iron and sulphur rich and lying in a bath of this muddy gunge is reputed to sooth the body, if not the soul.

GETTING THERE

Frequent buses from Ceske Budejovice, and meandering train if you've time for leisurely travel.

STAYING

Modest-priced rooms can be booked at the Bily; more expensive ones at Hotel Zlata hvezda (see Where To Drink below). B&B in private houses can be arranged through the local tourist information office at namesti Masarykovo 146, tel 0333-2557.

WHAT TO SEE

If you've come this far the brewery is well worth visiting if you can arrange it, but you need to organise a tour well in advance (see Breweries section). The anglicised name Regent comes from the founder of the hundreds of fish ponds and lakes which pepper the area. And, you've probably guessed it, he was one of the Rozmberk family. The oldest lakes date from the thirteenth century but most were created in the sixteenth, partly to drain the swampy land and partly to cater for the Bohemian taste for carp. One of the biggest lakes is on Trebon's doorstep, almost at the brewery gates – the Svet – where you can fish or hire sail or pedal boats. It's interesting to note that this naturally swampy countryside is more than 1,400 feet above sea level, way above the tree line in Britain.

The focal point of Trebon – former German name Wittingenau – is the traditionally Bohemian oblong town "square", namesti Masarykovo, which has recently been renovated and made traffic-free. The medieval layout which fans out from it is still partially surrounded by fortified walls, and the best place to see these is bordering the lake near the brewery. Trebon also has a castle, off the top end of the square, with an exhibition telling the story of the carp lake building. Traditionally, carp is eaten at Christmas and served with a sweetish dark sauce and Regent dark beer. Nowadays, more than half the annual carp catch is exported to Germany, where the Catholic Bavarians have similar tastes.

WHERE TO DRINK

HOSPUDKA NA MILERCE
Na Valech, or Valy, opposite Regent Brewery gates
🍺 *Regent pale 10*
🕐 *Daily 1000-2300*

A small, basic and cheerful bar where pool is fashionable. Opposite is an excellent beer restaurant, the Supina, specialising in local carp, plus Regent pale and dark 12.

HOTEL BILY KONICEK (White Horse)
Masarykovo namesti 27
Tel 0333-2818
🍺 *Regent pale 12 and Samson pale 10*
🕐 *Daily 1000-2200*

An old coaching inn built in 1570 and one of twenty-six that formed Regent's former tied estate before Communist nationalisation. Today, it is slowly breaking out from under its drab 1970s formica layer. In summer, its terrace is the best place to sit and enjoy the local beer and traffic-free town square scene. Rooms from 500 crowns (£12.50) a night.

HOTEL ZLATA HVEZDA (Golden Star)
Masarykovo namesti 107. Tel 0333-2661. Fax 0333-2604.
🍺 *Regent pale and dark 12*
🕐 *Daily 1000-2300*

Its more expensive than neighbouring outlets, but this is the place to eat the local carp. If you stay here, the family-owned hotel, formerly part of the Regent Brewery estate, will organise practically anything for you – from a mud health bath to a hot air balloon.

NEARBY

One of the most enchanting of Bohemian castles is north of Trebon. Cervena Lhota sits in the middle of a lake, although now connected by a bridge. The small, sixteenth-century castle is still painted a deep shade of pink (Cervena means red) supposedly to hide a scarlet cross left by the devil after he carried off some medieval owner's daughter who had renounced god. In the nearby village of Kardasova Recice the nameless pub on the main square serves Pilsner Urquell, Purkmistr dark and Gambrinus pale 10. Daily 1000-2200.

VESELI

STARA KRCMA
Main street through the town
🍺 *Samson 10 and 12 pale. Bottled Regent dark 12.*
🌓 *Daily 0900-2100*
Traditional town pub which has branched out into more adventurous catering, including seven ways of cooking carp from the surrounding lakes.

If you travel farther east from Trebon towards Moravia and Brno, the small town of Studena (60 km, 37 miles from Trebon) has a little state-owned brewery. It was founded in the early seventeenth century but there are doubts about it surviving the twentieth. Look for its scarce beers in U Javorice. Nearby the town of Telc ranks alongside Cesky Krumlov and Olomouc for architectural beauty. The large main square, bordered by gabled and arcaded houses of the Renaissance and Baroque periods, is ranked as the most stunning in the country. The old town centre, which includes a fifteenth-century castle and several authentic period pubs, is virtually surrounded by water which once formed part of the town's defences.

VYSOKY CHLUMEC

Here is one of the last bastions of Bohemian country brewing. Not only did the small, historic brewery (see Breweries) survive the purges of the Communist era but it has recently been reunited with the adjacent forested estate and castle under a restitution agreement with the aristocratic Lobkowiczy family who had owned all three since the early seventeenth-century until the Communist takeover in 1948.

The pretty village of Vysoky Chlumec is to be found (with difficulty on some maps) east of Breznice just off Route 18 between Pribram and Votice, near Sedlcany. Tours of the brewery are possible. Tel (within Prague) 2199-4111, fax (from UK) 0042-2-2199-4112.

Lobkowiczy beers can be drunk at Restaurace St. Hospoda (daily 1000-2200) near the castle, and in Sedlcany at U Marku, Komenskho namesti 48 (Mon-Fri 1000-2200, closed weekends).

PILSEN

Plzen – or Pilsen as it is known outside the Czech Republic – is probably the most famous brewing town on earth. For better or worse, and mostly the latter, breweries almost everywhere have poached Pilsen's name by producing beers with the Pilsner/Pilsener appellation.

It all stems from a group of burghers who got together in the town in 1839 to create a new brewery dedicated to the new bottom-fermentation brewing methods that had become all the rage across the border in Munich and Vienna. An accidentally unique combination of very soft local water, pale malt and Bohemian hops resulted in a beer which was soon in demand at royal courts as well as the local pubs. The concurrent development of the nearby spas of Marienbad (Marianske Lazne) and Karlsbad (Karlovy Vary), which attracted Europe's rich and famous, helped spread the new beer's fame abroad. Word got about among those who could afford to ponder such matters that a glass of Pilsner Urquell – first called Kaiserquell – possessed health-giving properties, an idea still propagated in Pilsen. Well, it certainly stimulates the gastric juices.

The founding fathers of Pilsner Urquell were descendants of some of the 260 burgher families granted individual brewing rights in perpetuity by King Wenceslas II when he gave the town its foundation charter in 1295. The impetus to build a new joint brewery in 1839 was partly driven by simmering dissatisfaction in the town with the variable quality of beer achieved by what had been until then traditional brewing methods – top-fermenting ale. The brewing burghers were stung into action after some of their number had been humiliated in 1838 when the local authorities publicly declared thirty-six barrels to be unfit for consumption and tipped the contents on to the main square outside the town hall.

The first batch of beer from the new Burgerliches Brauhaus, or Burghers' Brewery, was ready to drink at the town's Martinmas Fair in November 1842. Its unusually pale colour and clean, dry taste caused a sensation, and guest Bavarian brewer Josef Groll, 29, was the toast of the town.

The brewery that was to have such a world impact nevertheless had a modest beginning and in its first year produced less than fifty barrels a week. Today, using technology which makes traditionalists cringe, annual production is more than 1,125,000 hl (685,000 barrels).

In the 1990s, Urquell has been rediscovered by many Czechs who for the forty years of the Communist era were often denied it because much of the production was exported to earn foreign currency. It is now the third biggest-selling beer in the country, as well as being exported to fifty-two countries.

Pilsner Urquell is the flagship beer among the four breweries which now make up the privatised Pilsner Urquell Corporation, although Urquell's neighbouring brewery in Plzen, Gambrinus, produces the biggest-selling beer in the country. The other two breweries in the group are Domazlice and Karlovy Vary. A fifth, at Cheb on the Bavarian border, was closed in 1995. Other breweries that had been part of the original state-owned group, notably the now family-owned Chodova brewery, were able to cut loose and are still operating.

The Urquell Corporation produces 3.4 million hl (over 2 million barrels) a year and holds 18 per cent of the total Czech beer market. Its immediate ambition is to take 25 per cent of the market.

The heirs of those burghers who were given eternal brewing rights in 1295 now have a nice little earner. On privatisation in 1994, they were given a collective shareholding in the Urquell Corporation of 9.5 per cent.

The rest of the corporation is owned by several Czech investment groups. In an heroic attempt to protect the family silver, the government placed a five-year ban on the sale of any shareholding to foreign interests. This moratorium also includes restraints on sub-letting the Pilsner Urquell trademark abroad (brewing under licence). But vultures are patient: the moratorium ends in June 1999.

The runaway success of the new Burghers Brewery encouraged others in Pilsen to adopt bottom-fermentation techniques, and the old ale-producing ways were quickly doomed. Three more breweries were established but only Gambrinus (1868) has survived. The name of one of the others, Prior, was revived in 1995 in the shape of the Urquell Corporation's new wheat beer, brewed in Domazlice (see also Breweries chapter – Pilsner Urquell, Gambrinus, Domazlice, Karlovy Vary).

GETTING THERE

Express trains and buses connect with Prague's main train and bus stations and some German cities, notably Munich. The main railway station in Pilsen is a ten-minute walk from Pilsner Urquell's visitor entrance, which is near a busy junction of redeveloped roads. The bus station is farther away, on Husova, on the other side of the main square.

STAYING

There is a broad range of accommodation in Pilsen to suit most pockets. The Hotel Slovan (Smetanovy Sady 1, tel 019-33551) is a moderately priced, nineteenth-century building of some elegance in the city centre close to the main square. The Cedok travel office in Pilsen (tel 019-723517, fax 723624) can guide you to a selection of cheaper B&Bs. In the moderate price bracket, they recommend: Pension City, tel 019-222976; Pension Vion, tel 019-82582;

Pension Minihotel, tel-fax 019-8255.

What to See

The chief reason to visit Pilsen, unless you intend to buy a Skoda car, must be to drink at the font of just about the world's most famous brewery – and there are now two fonts (see Where To Drink). No one reading this book would trek to Pilsen just to take a peek at the Czech Republic's largest town square (namesti Republiky), whose four sides together measure more than one mile. But if you are visiting Pilsen, then the square is well worth seeing, as is the large genuinely gothic St. Bartholomew's Church (sv. Bartholomeje) in the middle. It boasts the tallest steeple (338 feet) in the country. The square is the architectural and cultural focal point of the city, which otherwise is a drab conurbation suffering all the usual late-twentieth century consequences of rapid industrial expansion and accompanying hurried building. The town took a serious beating in World War Two as Allied bombing tried to knock out the tank-making Skoda works. Although Pilsen had an industrial base at the end of the nineteenth century, there was a messy expansion of industry and population post-1948. The excellent Museum of Brewing (see below) adjoins the square, and a walk away on Tylova there is a museum dedicated to the history of the Skoda works, founded in 1866 by Emil von Skoda. Even in the nineteenth century it was the biggest armaments factory in the Hapsburg empire.

A steel foundry in Pilsen was used to make a British TV commercial in the early 1990s to promote a Yorkshire beer because Sheffield no longer had the capability to oblige.

The Urquell and Gambrinus breweries are across the River Radbuza, ten minutes' walk from the square. There are daily tours of Urquell, starting at the famous brewery arch on U Prazdroje. The tour – taken by 45,000 people in 1994 – includes the brewhouse and parts of the old fermentation and lagering cellars. By now, part of the 9 km (5 miles) of cellars and tunnels dug into the sandstone beneath the brewery may have been converted into a car park, where once the original Pilsner fermented and matured in giant oak tubs and barrels, drawing some of its special characteristics from the micro-climatic environment in that subterranean world. The 150 year-old practice ended in 1992 and with it the craft of maintaining the barrels and repitching their insides. The clinical, gleaming stainless steel replacement has all the lure and romance of a hospital operating theatre. It's possible that a small unit of the old system, due to be put back into operation during 1996, will be open to visitors, otherwise you will have to be contented with the brewery PR film or, better, try to see Michael Jackson's episode on Pilsen from his Beer Hunter TV series. The planned small-scale old system is to enable brewers and a chosen panel of local tasters to monitor the beer in its new environment, the company says. To book a tour place, contact Miss Krosva, tel 0042-19-706-2632, fax 706-2715.

MUSEUM OF BREWING (PIVOVARSKE MUZEUM V PLZNI)

Veleslavinova 6. Off the main square, namesti Republiky

Open Tues-Sun 1000-1800

Many European towns and cities with strong beery traditions boast museums dedicated to beer and brewing. They include Munich, Dortmund, Amsterdam, Copenhagen, and Burton. But the one in Pilsen claims to be the oldest; it is certainly one of the biggest and most colourful. A plan to open the museum was conceived in 1929 and the next ten years were spent bringing together exhibits. But World War Two intervened and it was 1959 before the museum formally opened. The museum building was for centuries a malthouse supplying Pilsen's medieval brewers. Later it became a brew pub and remained a "beer house" until the 1930s. The museum holds rare documents recording the history of brewing in the region; nineteenth-century brewing and malting equipment; pub furnishings and bric-a-brac from several centuries; and collections of beer mugs and brewery signs. But perhaps the most fascinating exhibit is a model steam brewery which is capable of producing 30 litres (52 pints). The technical curio has been exhibited at industrial shows in other parts of the world. The museum also tells the story, backed by documents and equipment, of the creation and early days of the brewery we now know as Pilsner Urquell, which created the first golden lager in 1842, as well as tracing the lives of Urquell's first brewers, in particular Bavarian Josef Groll who was invited to Pilsen by the brewery's founders to create the first brews. He was chosen because of his knowledge of the then new bottom-fermentation technique which would replace the dark, murky brews that had been standard fare for centuries. The museum, visited by 50,000 people a year, was renovated in 1991-92 under the sponsorship of the Pilsner Urquell group. Part of the building is styled like a medieval brewhouse. There is a semi-permanent exchange of exhibits between Pilsen and the Heineken brewery museum in Amsterdam.

WHERE TO DRINK

NA PARKANE

Veleslavinova (near the Museum of Brewing)

🍺 *Gambrinus 10, Purkmistr 10*

🕒 *Mon-Sat 0900-2200; Sun 1100-2100*

Cheerful locals' pub close to the main square and very handy for R&R after working up a thirst in the brewing museum along the street. Spruced up to lure the occasional tourist. Simple food fare to order.

U SALZMANNU

Prazska. Directly off the north-east corner of namesti Republiky

🍺 *Pilsner Urquell 12, Gambrinus 10, Purkmistr 10*

🕒 *Daily 1000-2200*

Probably the town's most noted traditional hostelry, catering for the comings and goings of a mix of city-centre shoppers, workers and visitors. Handy for regaining your equilibrium after falling dizzy while gazing up at the country's tallest church steeple (103 metres/338 feet) round the corner on the square.

NA SPILCE

In the Urquell brewery yard

🍺 *Urquell 12, Purkmistr 12*

🍺 *Mon-Sat 1000-2200; Sun 1100-2100*

The brewery's old maltings have been converted into a 500-seat beer hall, the biggest in the Czech Republic. Hot food and clinking glasses all day; only the oompah band seems to be missing.

POPOVICKA FORMANKA

Namesti Republiky

🍺 *Kozel pale 10 & 12, dark 10*

🍺 *Daily 1000-2200*

A new pub in an old setting and one of a growing number owned and managed by the Velke Popovice brewery, which says it plans to open more in Pilsen. This one stays true to the character of a typical Czech hostelry: beer, solid hot meals and animated chatter.

U ZUMBERG

Bezrucova. One block south of the main square

🍺 *Gambrinus 10 and 12*

🍺 *Mon-Sat 0900-2200; closed Sunday.*

A simple watering hole popular with workers in blue overalls whose pockets have convinced them that no beer comes better than Gambrinus 10, the most popular brew in Pilsen, Bohemia, the Czech Republic...

PILSNER URQUELL ORIGINAL RESTAURANT

Beside the famous brewery arch entrance to Urquell brewery, U Prazdroje 7

🍺 *Urquell 12, Gambrinus 10 and 12, Purkmistr 12, Prior*

🍺 *Mon-Sat 1000-2200; closed Sunday*

The second in the planned chain of look-alike corporate Urquell pubs, all selling the group's premium products (12 degree beers). This one opened in autumn 1995 in the converted beer restaurant-cum-beer hall which had for years been a haunt of workers and brewery visitors. The first in the chain opened in the spa town of Karlovy Vary (Karlsbad) in 1994. Prague and Brno were due to be next in the chain during 1996. By Czech pub standards they are upmarket and reminiscent of a Munich beer restaurant – chunky scrubbed wood furnishings, brewery bric-a-brac and swirling waiters and waitresses dressed in severe black and white uniforms. The beer quality is good – as it should be – and traditional Bohemian dishes are served up all day.

NORTH BOHEMIA

Unlike south Bohemia, which is primarily rural, north Bohemia is a mixture of delightful castle-strewn, forested countryside, hop fields, and ugly industrial towns surrounded by the scars of open-cast mining. Brown coal was one of the main sources of industrial and domestic fuel in the country during the forty-year Communist era. The entire town of Most, including a fifteenth-century brewery, was demolished in the late 1960s to get at a rich seam of the coal just below the surface. Conversely, the countryside around Zatec is blessed with rich red loam which nurtures the world-famous Bohemian hop. And further west, densely wooded hillsides and valleys provide the backdrop to the spas of Karlovy Vary and Marianske Lasne – known to older generations as Karlsbad and Marienbad.

Until recent times, many of the rural communities along the border region skirting Germany had centuries-old traditions of brewing, and busy breweries flourished in almost every village – just as in neighbouring Bavaria today. In 1947 there were forty-one breweries in west Bohemia. In the Chodova district alone there were brewhouses at Tachov, Stod, Stankov, Loket, Radnice, and Plasy. But although the Communist era preserved classical Czech methods of brewing – primarily, one suspects, because they didn't have the money to do otherwise – the dogmatic centralised planning had much the same effect as capitalism's notorious "economies of scale" and many little breweries disappeared. After the first euphoria of unshackled brewing in the early 1990s, the closures resumed in 1995 when the privatised Pilsner Urquell Corporation deemed Cheb's last brewery to be surplus to its increasingly centralised production. Brewing had been going on in Cheb since 1300.

On the brighter side, there are still thirty-one breweries across northern Bohemia – from Chodova Plana in the west to Nachod in the east.

According to the latest official figures, brewing continues in: Belec nad Orlici (new micro), Broumov, Chodova Plana, Decin, Dobruska, Golcuv Jenikov, Hlinsko, Hradec Kralove, Karlovy Vary, Klaster Hradiste, Kutna Hora, Lanskroun, Liberec, Litomerice, Louny, Maly Rohozec, Most, Nachod, Nova Paka, Nymburk, Pardubice, Podkovan, Policka, Rakovnik/Krusovice (2), Svijany, Svitavy, Trutnov, Usti nad Labem, Velke Brezno, Zatec. Many of these breweries are now privately owned, some are still held by the state and awaiting buyers. The future for most of them is tough and many will not survive into the new century. A few have foreign backing and will prosper. In addition, several other new micro-breweries are reported to have begun operating (see Micros chapter).

The places detailed below are in alphabetical order.

CHODOVA PLANA

Blink and you'll miss it, but behind this one-street village south of Marianske on the Pilsen-Cheb route 21 road, is the last of many small family breweries which used to pepper this border country region.

The now privatised, 420 year-old Chodovar brewery (see Breweries – Chodovar) survived several plans during the Communist era to close it, and because of its small size was surplus to the requirements of the managers at Pilsner Urquell and Gambrinus in Pilsen with which it had been lumped during the nationalised era. The brewery was bought by the Plevka family, which had been associated with it for many years. The new chairman, Jiri Plevka senior, was about to retire after thirty years as manager at Chodovar when he and his sons Jiri and Jan and brother-in-law Milan made the decision to bid for it. "I had worked too much in the past to stop it closing", said the chairman, "so I had to postpone my place in the sun."

Chodovar beers, including an unfiltered pale 10 and delicious dark, are in pubs in Tachov, Marianske Lazne and the Cheb district.

A good best place to try the beers locally is in adjoining Plana, a pretty village off the main Pilsen-Cheb route 21 road. At the time of writing, one of the village's ancient pubs was closed for renovation, but the basic, gnarled Cerny Medved (Black Bear) was in business (daily 0900-2130). In Tachov, drink Chodovar beers at the Lidovy Dum (Mon-Fri 0900-2200, Sat 0800-1400).

KARLOVY VARY (Karlsbad)

The water of this handsome spa town is far better known than the local brewery's beer, although in the nineteenth century it was fashionable for kings, emperors and their followers to take the hot spring waters by day and sup Pilsner Urquell by night – or the much stronger Becherovka, a locally-produced, herb-based liqueur sometimes referred to as the "thirteenth spring" (there are about sixty hot springs in and around Karlovy, but only a dozen are in commercial use). All these liquids were believed by the hoi polloi of the times to have health-giving properties. Today, the health-giving benefits of an up-market tourist industry are being felt by local entrepreneurs as the town wipes the long sleep from its eyes and resumes its rightful role, persuading wealthy people to drink or wallow in the foul tasting, warm, salty and sulphurous local spring waters. So it's not surprising that Urquell chose Karlovy Vary as the place to launch its planned new chain of twenty-five corporate pubs-cum-beer restaurants. But of the produce of Pivovar Karlovy Vary – part of the Pilsner Urquell group – there is little outward sign. You have to delve into the grubbier, high-rise suburbs to find the locally popular Karel IV, a fruity, crisp beer named after Holy Roman Emperor Charles IV who allegedly discovered the spa's hot springs while out hunting one fine day in 1348 – the same year he also established central Europe's first university, in Prague. Busy man. With tourists returning in greater numbers, all the major brewers are jostling to ply their wares on the main, pedestrianised street where people promenade, sipping the spa waters and munching cream cakes. The brewers are also keen to ensure that they are represented in the most un-spa-like annual Beer Olympiad, a sort of beer-drinking athletics. A popular event invites contestants to drink a half litre while standing on their heads – current world record 9.4 seconds. The Olympiad takes place during May. Another annual event which might not have met with the approval of former regular royal visitors is the Miss Czech Beauty Competition. Call the local tourist office for exact dates (see Staying below).

GETTING THERE

Regular bus services from Florenc Bus Station in Prague. The journey takes nearly three hours, but a day return trip is possible. Regular buses also from Pilsen. The train takes about a week via Zatec and all points, but is very scenic. By car from Prague the most direct route is 130 km (81 miles).

STAYING

There is plenty of accommodation, ranging from rooms in private houses to the Grand Hotel Pupp at 4,000 crowns (£100). The tourist information office is in the garish 1970s Communist building which encompasses one of the spa spouts: Vridelni kolonada, tel 017-24097, fax 24667.

WHAT TO SEE

Although the town was allegedly founded in the mid-fourteenth century as a spa, most of the visually attractive Karlovy Vary dates from the nineteenth century. The architectural legacy of that spa boom period flanks both sides of a small river flowing down the main street, which becomes narrower and more steep-sided as you walk up from the bus station towards the Grand Hotel Pupp, whose former guests include Russian Czars and Austrian Emperor Franz Josef. Some of the grand hotels and houses which once catered for Europe's rich are now workers' tenement blocks with faded facades; others are shuttered pending restitution legalities; some like the Astoria (art nouveau) have been returned to their full beauty. Several spa fonts, called colonnades, are dotted along the river street, which is mostly pedestrianised. The way to work up a thirst is to buy a traditional long-spouted cup at one of these fonts and sip one of the salty spa waters as you promenade. Churches of different style and persuasion dot the district as testament to the spiritual needs of the different nationalities who converged on Karlovy for the season. The Anglican red-brick church is close to the Russian Orthodox place of worship, modelled on a Moscow church. More recent Russian influences include the Yuri Gagarin Colonnade and a statue of Karl Marx (opposite the tourist office at the Vridelni-Gagarin colonnade), if it hasn't been torn down as in most other towns and cities of central-eastern Europe. But Karl's link with Karlsbad is more than just political: he came here several times in the mid-1870s.

WHERE TO DRINK

Many of the drinking places in the centre offer Pilsner Urquell ... or Pilsner Urquell

PILSNER URQUELL ORIGINAL RESTAURANT

I.P. Pavlova 8 (the main street) between hotels Patria & Otava

🍺 *Urquell 12, Purkmistr 12, Prior wheat*

🕐 *Daily 1100-2300*

The first of a planned twenty-five or more brewery-owned or controlled beer restaurants. It's intended that they will have a corporate identity. The style is comfortably unfussy and Bavarian-like with lots of wood panelling, chunky wood furniture, tiled floors and brewery bric-a-brac on the walls. They are not aimed at your average Czech, in fact the Urquell Corporation wants to extend the chain to foreign cities such as Vienna. Traditional Czech dishes and busy waiters.

KAVARNA VALENCIA

I.P. Pavlova, opposite the Muhlbrunnen Colonnade

🍺 *Krusovice pale and dark 12*

🕐 *Daily 1100-2100*

Not your typical Czech drinking haunt, but the beer's worth trying.

KRASNA KRALOVNA (NICE QUEEN)

I.P. Pavlova

🍺 *Staropramen pale 12*

🕐 *Mon-Sat 1200-2300; Sunday 1400-2200*

Glitzy little bar at the top end of main street on the bend opposite the sprawling Grand Hotel Pupp.

PIVNICE CERNA PLZEN

Moskevska 50

🍺 *Karel 11 pale, Primus 10 pale*

🕐 *Daily 1000-2200*

A bustling locals' pub away from the tourist tracks. Down-to-earth cooking.

NEARBY

The village of Loket about 8 km (5 miles) south-west of Karlovy Vary has an impressively large, 700 year-old fortified castle. It's built on a steep river gorge and was part of Bohemia's medieval defences against intruding armies. Beds and Karlovy Vary beer are available at the Bily Kun in the village.

KUTNA HORA

65 km (40 miles) East of Prague

A large, unusually designed Gothic church, built with silver miners' money, is the reason most people make the journey from Prague to this small, pretty town. Some people think the Church of St. Barbara is more impressive than Prague's cathedral. The Kutna Hora church has three tent-like towers and exceptionally ornate flying buttresses. St. Barbara is the patron saint of miners, and silver was mined here for the royal Bohemian mint for about 450 years until the mid-1800s. The town's former wealth is also reflected in a variety of rich Gothic, Renaissance and Baroque architecture, and a museum of mining in Barborska street tells the whole digging story.

The miners' thirst was also taken very good care of down the centuries, and today's small brewery – still partially owned by the town – can trace its history on the same site back to

1573.

The brewery (210,000 hl;, 127,000 barrels) is part of the Bohemia Breweries group which is increasingly concentrating on a new brand – Old Bohemia. But Kutna Hora still produces several local beers, notably Kutnohorske pale 10, and a dark 10 beer dedicated to the by-gone miners, Kutnohorsky Havir (Kutna Hora Miner). Places to toast the miners include: U Hvairu (daily 1000-2200) and U Moroveho sloupu (Mon-Sat 1100-2200) both on Sultyskovo namesti.

There are frequent trains and buses from Prague.

LIBEREC

North-east of Prague

In the vicinity of this border textile town there were two old-established breweries until about 1991. The one at Jablonec closed then but the property is believed to have been sold as a brewing concern and may yet re-open. The other brewery, at Vratislavice nad Nisou, was bought by Bass in late 1995 and seems to have relatively secure prospects.

Vratislavice has been privatised since 1992 and was one of the most successful medium sized breweries (500,000 hl; 300,000 barrels) in Bohemia before Bass acquired a 55 per cent shareholding in October 1995. The brewery's export markets were badly affected when neighbouring Poland introduced stiff import tariffs in 1993. Its premium pale beer is known in some British supermarkets as Vratislav Lager. It remains to be seen whether Bass will promote this further or concentrate on the Czech domestic market. The Vratislavice company also owns the smaller brewery at Svijany, to the south-west, and its future could be in doubt. Vratislavice beers are widely available in the Liberec district.

Liberec has been making cloth since it was founded by German immigrants in the middle ages; it used to be called Reichenberg and there are still German speakers in the area. It has an architecturally attractive old centre and, inevitably, a castle.

Vratislavice nad Nisou was the birthplace of Ferdinand Porsche, the car maker, in 1875.

Direct train and bus routes from Prague.

LITOMERICE

North of Prague

Apart from a state-owned brewery, this town has a well-preserved medieval town centre the focal point of which is the main square, featuring Gothic, Renaissance and Baroque architecture. The cash-strapped brewery dates from the eighteenth century but was rebuilt in the 1920s. Its chief beer is a pale 11 called Kalich, which is on sale in most of Litomerice's pubs.

The town is on a direct bus route from Prague, or via Louny.

Nearby: in 1995 an old brewery was being renovated in Teplice, part of the restituted estate of the aristocratic Lobkowicz family (see South Bohemia, Breweries chapters).

MARIANSKE LAZNE (Marienbad)

West of Prague

One of the Czech Republic's two main spas, Marianske is smaller, less gaudy and more green than its neighbour Karlovy Vary (45 km; 28 miles distant) but has a much more impressive central spa building, the ornate wrought iron Colonnade. The town is more open, less clustered than Karlovy. It is also recovering its economic equilibrium more slowly. But in its nineteenth-century hey-day, Marianske's forty-two salty and sulphurous springs were as attractive to the wealthy hypochondriacs as anywhere else with a fashionable "cure". Marianske's waters are reputed to be particularly good for treating obesity and ailments of the bladder, kidneys, stomach, and skin, as well as settling your nerves. Among the regulars were Britain's King Edward VII and his relation Tsar Nicholas II. The town's eighteen-hole golf course was formally opened by Edward in 1905. There's a Dick Whittington story associated with Marianske: the humble gardener Vaclav Skalnik, responsible for transforming the bogs which oozed the sulphur springs into pretty gardens in the early nineteenth century, rose to become town mayor. A more recent attraction is the singing fountain in front of the Colonnade, which is programmed to put on a performance of varying water sprays in time to classical music. The locals could be forgiven for preferring to indulge the excellent beers of the Chodova Plana brewery, 10 km (6 miles) down the road, which compete more or less successfully with the bigger brewers' fare. The town's information office is on Hlavni trida, tel 0165-5346

GETTING THERE

A regular bus service runs from Pilsen (66 km; 41 miles) via the brewery town of Chodova Plana,

and there are several buses a day from Prague.

WHERE TO DRINK

JIZERKA
Tyrsova 44, off Hlavni trida
🍺 *Chodova pale 12 and dark 10. Gambrinus 10*
🕐 *Daily 1100-2200*
One of the new breed of Czech pubs, this one has an anglers' theme with hanging nets and other appurtenances. There's a big, modestly-priced fish menu, including pike, which matches the dark beer.

NADRAZI BUFET
(Railway station buffet)
Husova
🍺 *Chodova pale 10*
🕐 *Daily 0800-2100*
The cheapest beer and food in town served up in a 1950s cafeteria. The soups are a meal in themselves.

CHURCHILL RESTAURANT
Hotel Excelsior, Hlavni trida
🍺 *Urquell 12, Purkmistr 12*
🕐 *Daily 1100-2200*
A smart beer restaurant in an very up-market hotel.

NEARBY

East of Marianske Lazne is the beautiful, twelfth-century Tepla Monastery (buses run from Marianske), whose brothers created the spa in 1808 on land they owned. They collected lucrative rent until the Communist takeover, when the monastery, which also had its own brewery, was closed down and turned into an army barracks. In 1995 there was talk of the monks starting brewing again.

Half way between Marianske and Karlovy, castle lovers should see the impressive Renaissance stronghold perched on a hill overlooking the handsome village of Becov, where the Hubertus pub on the main square offers Staropramen beers and bed and breakfast.

Most

Most is a must for environmentalists. A huge open-cast mining crater exists today where once stood the old Gothic town, including a fifteenth-century brewery. The town was demolished during the 1960s and early 1970s so that brown coal just below the surface could be mined to fuel the burgeoning chemical industry. The population was moved to high-rise flats built nearby. The only building to survive the demolition was a sixteenth-century church. The tower was dismantled stone by stone and rebuilt and the rest of the structure, weighing 12,000 tonnes, was literally lifted with jacks and moved half a mile.

A new brewery was built in the early 1970s and because of its comparatively good condition quickly found a buyer after the end of state control. It was taken over by Radegast in 1995 and is now brewing Radegast beers for the Prague market.

Nachod

Although close to the Polish border in far-flung, north-east Bohemia, Nachod is a brewing curio worth a visit if time permits. It is the only place left in this part of Europe where the town owns the local brewery.

Before the Communist takeover of 1948 – which technically resulted in everything in the country being owned by "the people" – Nachod's town council had been the brewery owners. After the collapse of Communism in 1989, the newly-elected council negotiated the restitution of the brewery to the town (see Breweries chapter).

Nachod brewery shares pride of place with a sixteenth-century castle perched on a hill overlooking the town. It houses a big art collection. For history buffs, another notable castle 8 km (5 miles) west of Nachod is at Ratiborice, where the Russian Tsar Alexander I met Prussian and Austrian leaders in 1813 to plot joint action to put an end to Napoleon's conquest of Europe.

Nachod's other claim to fame is being twinned with Warrington; a pity then that the Cheshire town's brewing industry has all but ceased to exist.

Getting There

There are regular bus and train services through the day from Prague.

Staying

Pension Oase (tel 0441-23435) and Pension Komfort (tel 0441-21584) have reasonably priced rooms with breakfast. The tourist information office has a bigger list of accommodation. Call 0441-23828 or fax 0441-23751.

Where To Drink

Hotel Hynek
Ceskoskalicka 17
🍺 *Primator Premium and Primator Dark*
🕐 *Daily 1000-2200*

One of the more salubrious drinking places in town, catering for a broad mix of people.

SAVENA

Potraviny in the Kamenice district of the town,
- *Primator Light (pale 10)*
- *Mon-Fri 0900-2200; Sat-Sun 1000-2200*

A typical locals' pub. Lively early evenings. Hot and cold dishes.

NEARBY

There is a co-operative brewery in Hradec Kralove. At Trutnov, the local private brewery has begun specialising in unfiltered beers. One of its employees in Communist times was the country's current playwright-president Vaclav Havel, sent there as "penance" for his human rights campaigns. The Communists seem not to have appreciated that Havel is a keen beer drinker. Look for Trutnov's Krakonos brands in the Varsava (daily 0900-2130). Brew-pubs have sprung up in Hradec Kralove, and 8 km east at Belec nad Orlici, and at the U Lipy in Svinistany between Jaromer and Nachod (see Micros chapter).

RAKOVNIK

This historic country town 50 km (31 miles) west of Prague boasts two breweries – Krusovice and Pivovar Rakovnik, which is part of the private Bohemia Breweries Prague group. The oldest of the two is Krusovice which was once linked with the nearby former royal Krivoklat Castle, one of the oldest surviving fortified castles in Bohemia, which towers over the surrounding forests.

Since 1994 Krusovice has been 51 per cent owned by the giant German brewing group Binding and under the Germans' marketing tutelage it has given itself the grandiose title Kralovsky Krusovice – Royal Brewery Krusovice plc (see Breweries chapter).

Some of the local beers can be sampled at the Druzba (daily 1000-2300) in Rakovnik. In the little village beside the castle, U Dvoraku offers Krusovice beers (daily 1000-2300). A regular bus service connect Prague with Rakovnik. Trains from Prague's Smichov station go closer to Krivoklat Castle, which is closed on Mondays.

NEARBY

The most famous and perhaps also most spectacular castle in Bohemia, Karlstejn, is 27 km (17 miles) south-east of Krivoklat, via Beroun which until recently had a brewery (see Prague chapter, What To See).

ZATEC

The town stands on a hill like a sentinel guarding the surrounding ancient hop fields for which Bohemia is famous. And to underline Zatec's bond with the climbing plant which has been an ingredient of the brewers' art for almost 1,000 years, a small symbolic hop garden holds pride of place on the main square where other towns might erect a statue to some civic worthy or war hero. Zatec has clearly seen better days but the town recognises that its wealth and prosperity has for centuries been linked to the production and export of the Bohemian hop – better known abroad by its German name,

Saaz.

Today, the main hop-processing businesses are still based in Zatec, although in the mid-1990s the trickle down effect of the economic regeneration resulting from the "Velvet Revolution" of 1989 had barely reached this northern market town. The first outward sign of improvement anywhere in the Czech Republic always seems to be the town square, and in 1995 Zatec's was receiving its face lift. In the same year, the brewery which in 1989 had a death sentence hanging over it, was sold into private ownership with plans for modernisation (see Breweries chapter Zatec).

Zatec and district had a large German population until the ethnic cleansing of the mid-1940s. The medieval humanist writer Johannes von Saaz – author of Der Ackermann aus Bohmen/The Ploughman from Bohemia – was town clerk in the late 1300s, and one of the instigators of the German peasant wars, Thomas Muntzer, lived here.

GETTING THERE

Trains run from Prague and Pilsen but they take for ever. Buses link with the town from Prague via Louny, and there is a service direct from Pilsen en route to Most.

STAYING

There are several B&B places. Enquire at the information office in the town hall. Hotels/pensions of variable standard and price include: Druzba, Zlaty lev and Zlaty Andel (the cheapest).

WHAT TO SEE

Zatec is still partially surrounded by medieval town walls and the traditionally elongated square is flanked by arcades and attractively gabled houses. In late 1995 the square and many of its buildings were being renovated. A symbolic hop garden (see above) has pride of place beside the town hall. The yellow stuccoed twin towers of the fourteenth-century Church of Assumption indicate the way to Zatec's brewery which has been painted pastel pink. One of the ancient town gates (Knezka brana), adjacent to the church, offers sweeping views over the hop plains below.

WHERE TO DRINK

At the time of writing much of the town centre was being renovated and a number of old pubs were closed, either for repairs or because of ownership problems.

OAZA
Main square, adjacent to twin towered church
🍺 *Zatecka Desitka, Lucan, and Krusovice pale 10*
🕐 *Daily 1130-2300*
Small, dark modern bar close to the brewery.

RESTAURACE NA BASTE
Dvorakova, off main square
🍺 *Urquell 12, Purkmistr 12*
🕐 *Daily 1000-2200*
Modernised beer restaurant with friendly waiters and the biggest and best bramboraky in Bohemia.

RESTAURACE VACLAVKA
Obloukova 5

🍺 *Zatec's three beers on draught.*

🌑 *Mon-Sat 1000-2200; closed Sunday.*

Lively, modernised beer restaurant offering solid Bohemian dishes to accompany the local hoppy brews.

NEARBY

20 km (12 miles) north-east of Zatec is the brewery town of Louny, noted for quite hoppy beers, and an unusual Gothic church. St. Nicholas's has a rare spire with four pinnacles as well as a tent-like roof. Sample the local beer in the Union Hotel.

A few kilometres south of Zatec is the small town of Mecholupy, whose German name Michelob was adopted by American Budweiser brewers Anheuser-Busch for another of their mass market products.

There are castles at Citoliby, Peruc and Hazmburk.

Floor maltings at Cerna Hora

BRNO

The second largest Czech city is also the capital of Moravia, the eastern region of the ancient "Czech lands", which has its own ancient customs and traditions distinct from Bohemia. These may have been blurred during the Communist era, but now there is an attempt to redefine a cultural identity and heritage, if only to boost tourism. Folk music survives in place of the ubiquitous oompah band. One thing which visibly sets Moravia apart from Bohemia is the vineyards. Cultivation of the grape here is probably as old as that of the grain, but the vines, which produce pleasant light dry white wine, are in need of rejuvenation.

If Bohemia is famous for its hops then Moravia is the country's granary. South of Brno, the vineyards may stretch out towards the Austrian border, but to the north waving fields of barley greet the traveller; soil and continental climate conspire to produce some of the best brewing barley in Europe. The Czech Republic's chief maltings are at Prostejov, 50 kms (31 miles) north-east of Brno. But in the mid-1990s, a number of Moravian breweries still operated their own maltings, some even still using the ancient malt shovel. It's not surprising, then, that the Moravians' thirst for beer matches their Bohemian cousins. Perhaps more surprising is the fact that the first brewers' guild in central Europe was founded in Brno in 1353. In 1995, there were about thirty breweries in operation in the region, ranging from the Pegas brew pub in Brno to the expanding giant Radegast at Nosovice in Frydek-Mistek. Hops are also grown in Moravia's rich, dark loam in the Olomouc-Prostejov region.

Brno is a self-sufficient, self-contained city. Perhaps it was too insular once: this is where the father of genetics worked out the Theory of Heredity Inheritance. But the discovery by an obscure nineteenth-century monk Gregor Johann Mendel, while cultivating peas in a monastery garden next to the brewery, was ignored by the outside world for nearly half a century. Brno's other modern claim to fame is as the home of the Bren machine gun, one of the major small arms of the British Army during World War Two. The Bren takes its name from the first two letters of Brno – where it was designed and first made in the early 1930s – and Enfield, England, where it was later mass produced.

Some travel guides paint a falsely pessimistic picture of Brno as a grubby industrial town. Few late twentieth-century conurbations of 390,000 people would be without some grubby industry, but Brno is more charming than Birmingham, or Bradford, or Basingstoke. It has an old, dilapidated, but attractive centre of alarmingly quiet streets lined with nineteenth-century neo-Gothic buildings, reflecting Brno's past success as a textile town, and squares peppered with renaissance and baroque architecture. Strolling pedestrians are troubled only by trams. Traffic is mostly kept outside a ring of gardens replacing once massive fortification which held marauding seventeenth-century Tatar and Turkish armies at bay. A renovated thirteenth-century castle stands guard over the centre; thickly forested hills rise in the background; the trade fair grounds house some well kept Art Deco buildings which expressed new Czechoslovakia's national independence in the 1920s; and the yellow-stuccoed Starobrno wafts its malty aromas around.

Today, Brno is feeling its way into the outside world at a slower pace than Prague but helped along by being home to the country's biggest trade exhibition grounds which stages a spring brewing industry fair, Pivex. At the beginning of the 1990s, there were only two beers generally available in Brno, Starobrno pale and Starobrno dark, but today pubs offer plenty of out-of-town choice, restaurants are discovering new flavours, and nightlife is awakening from a long sleep, helped by a big university student population. The city's only major brewer, Starobrno, now has a majority Austrian shareholder, but it was so dilapidated and strapped for cash the alternative might have been closure (see Breweries - Starobrno).

For military historians, 20 km (12 miles) east of Brno at Slavkov u Brna (see Brno District chapter) is the scene of the Battle of Austerlitz where in 1805 Napoleon's Frenchmen destroyed the Russian and Austrian armies and confirmed his supremacy. More than 30,000 soldiers were killed.

GETTING THERE

Brno is linked to Prague (225 kms, 140 miles) by train and one of the country's busiest stretches of motorway, the D1 (E50). Trains are leisurely; they take about three hours to do the 225 km (140 mile) journey from the main Prague station. Buses are faster, more frequent and cheaper. They depart from the Florenc bus station – see Prague chapter.

STAYING

There is generally plenty of accommodation – and you can even stay above a brewery (see Pegas) – except during trade fair weeks when there is heavy demand for beds and prices rise by up to one third. The biggest fairs are held in spring and autumn. Some hotels charge less at weekends. If you arrive in Brno without accommodation, the local Cedok tourist office is in a modern single storey building opposite the railway station on Nadrazni. If you are on a strict budget, they can find rooms in private houses, or point you towards the nearest camp site. See Before You Start for Cedok's UK office. Here's a selection; prices for a double room with breakfast.

Hotel Pegas

This must be the best bet for a beer tour – modern rooms directly above Brno's only brew pub, and in the middle of the old town centre. Doubles at £35 are reduced to £25 Friday-Sunday, except during trade fair weeks. There are only a few rooms, so book in advance if possible. Jabuska 4, 602 00 Brno. Tel 05/422-10104, fax 05-422-14314.

Hotel Imos

A beer restaurant with modest, decent rooms, but away from the town centre. £40. Hudcova 72, 621 00 Brno. Tel 05-412-12354, fax 05-412-12351.

Hotel Slavia

An old-established hotel which still has an air of 1970s Communism trying to be trendy, such as a bar with an electric organ. Renovated with formica. Ten minutes walk from the railway station. 80 rooms with bathroom. Comfortable but expensive. £60. Solnicni 15, 622 16 Brno. Tel 05-23711, fax 24179.

Getting Around

Trams criss-cross the city and virtually all of them pass through the square in front of the railway station, where you can change money outside normal banking hours. The bus station for out-of-town trips to Olomouc etc. is behind the railway station off Plotni, reached via a pedestrian catwalk, or trams 5 and 19. Trams rides cost six crowns each.

What to See

Castle (hrad Spilberk)

Worth the climb for views over the city and a tour of fifteenth-century dungeons used by despots down the ages to lock up and torture opponents. Napoleon's armies were the first to crack its fortifications.

Old Town

The streets and squares on the hillock around the twin-spired St. Peter and Paul Cathedral are slowly being renovated and still retain a medieval air. There's a high density of bars and pubs here too, and the nearest thing to a curry house this far east (the Aladdin) on Dominikanske namesti. Churchgoers who hear the noon bells chime at 11am are not going mad; it's been going on ever since the townsfolk beat off a marauding protestant Swedish army in the seventeenth century. The Swedes promised to give up their week-long siege if they couldn't take the town by noon the next day, so the defenders rang the bells an hour early and the Swedes packed up and went home.

Trade Fair Grounds (Vystaviste)

If you like architecture, the grounds are full of Art Deco, built to celebrate the first ten years of Czechoslovakia's independence from the Austrian Hapsburgs. If you visit in early March, some of the buildings will be full of free beer, courtesy of the annual Pivex beer industry fair. It's open to the public for a modest charge, and if that's not enough the organisers let locals in free on one day of the week-long event. By 5pm there are more drunks than at the Munich

Oktoberfest. Trams 1, 18, 20 from the railway station.

MENDEL MUSEUM

Readers who remember school science may spot the significance of Mendlova namesti, where the Starobrno tap stands. The square is named after Gregor Johann Mendel, the father of modern genetics who first discovered hereditary inheritance in living things. In the 1850s in the former Augustinian monastery gardens adjacent to the brewery, he cultivated and tested 28,000 pea plants to reach his conclusions. Sadly for him, his discoveries went unheeded in the scientific world until long after his death. It was the 1920s before the significance of his work was recognised. The monastery is now a museum of Mendel's work.

WHERE TO DRINK

CERNOHORSKA PIVNICE

Kapucinske namesti 1
Old town centre near railway station
🍺 *Cerna Hora pale and dark 10 and 12*
🕒 *Mon-Fri 0800-2200; Sat 0900-1800; Sun 1500-2200*

It claims to be a beer cellar dating from the seventeenth century, but recent renovations have given it a very twentieth-century look, apart from the stumps of polished wood lagering barrels which line both sides of the cavernous room.

MORAVASKA CHALUPA,

Adjoins the 1,000-bed Hotel Voronez,
Krizkovskeho 47.
Buses 44, 84
🍺 *Starobrno pale 12*

🕒 *Tues-Sun 1700-2400; closed Mondays.*

A smart pub-restaurant which is popular for its traditional Moravian food and is kept busy during exhibitions at the nearby trade fair grounds.

PEGAS

Jabuska 4, 602 00 Brno. Tel 05/422-10104, fax 05-422-14314.
In a small narrow street off the main pedestrianised thoroughfare Ceska in the old town. Ten minutes walk from the railway station.
🍺 *Pegas pale and dark 12, wheat and ginger beers; all unfiltered.*
🕒 *Daily 1000-2400*

A long, narrow beer hall with a micro brewery in the middle that opened in 1992 and has been crowded ever since. Some of the most distinctive beers in town are to be found here, drunk by some of Brno's most discerning and enthusiastic drinkers. The private owners have fashioned a modern-day version of an ancient town inn: food, drink and lodging under one roof. The beer is brewed in the basement, it's drunk on the ground floor and, if need be, the guests – or at least some of them – can sleep it off upstairs. Bushy-bearded brewer Vladimir Stejskal has the enthusiasm to be innovative while at the same time providing the staple pale and dark beers. So far, he has produced a wheat beer and a refreshing bottom-fermented ginger beer, with ginger root powder replacing some of the traditional hop content. Its dry, slightly peppery flavour makes it a delightful aperitif, which is what he was aiming for. Vladimir, who trained at the Cena Hora brewery 25 kms north of Brno, is a purist who frowns on some of his customers' preference for a Rezane pivo – half and half of pale and dark. He doesn't think much of filtration either: "It deprives beer of many good qualities of taste and nutrients." That view is clearly shared by Pegas customers. Vladimir brews about 3,000 barrels a year. Some of the beer is sold to other pubs in the area, but most of it is drunk in-house – about 2,000 pints a day. With such a through-put, Pegas brews every day, and pressure of space means that most beer is matured for just twenty-one days following a six-day fermentation. Many 1990s European brew pubs seem to sell "green" (immature) beer, but the Pegas products don't taste that way. Vlad the Very Bearded uses only pelletised Zatec hops and four different Czech malts. A huge cross section of Brno-ites, as well as out-of-town trade fair exhibitors with their ear to the ground, frequent Pegas, and by late afternoon there is often standing room only. The brew pub caters for all-comers, and a few misguided souls do drop in for a coffee or even tea – served continental style in a glass, of course. But such customers are apt to attract funny looks, not least from the brewer.

PIVOVARSKA PIVNICE
Mendlova namesti, Stare Brno
Trams 1,6,9,14,18
🍺 *Starobrno pale 10 and 12, dark 10*
🕐 *Daily 0800-2200*
A cavernous basic boozer attached to the brewery but no longer owned by it, although dressed in the same yellow stuccoed coat. It's only the frequent movement in and out by blue-overalled men that indicates this might be a pub; there is no sign, welcoming or otherwise.

RESTAURACE BOVAUR
Junction of Pekarska and Uvoz (opposite monastery church, near Starobrno brewery)
🍺 *Krusovice pale 12 and dark 10*
🕐 *Daily 1000-2300*
A modern white table-clothed basement pub offering little in the way of atmosphere but a good lunchtime menu.

STOPKOVA
Ceska 5 (pedestrianised street in the old town centre)
🍺 *Pilsner Urquell and Purkmistr dark*
🕐 *Daily 1100-2300*
This is a traditional beer "hall" – long and narrow with grubby tables and whitewashed walls – which seems to acquire a preponderance of tired and emotional locals after 9pm. Some of them are not averse to slapping their womenfolk and sending them home, unless I was witnessing some other ancient local ritual. The beer's good, the food is cheap and plain, the piped musak and gaming machines haven't yet arrived, and the waiters liven up when they spot a foreigner, hopefully a generous German-speaking one. More pricey meals from the same kitchen are served on cleaner tables in the Stopkova restaurant on the first floor, but you can't slap women up there.

U SVATA JAKUBA
Jakubske namesti
Old town centre
🍺 *Starobrno pale 10 and 12*
🕐 *Daily 1100-2300*
An up-market pub in a small hotel of the same name offering the local beer plus good quality Czech cuisine at reasonable prices. Close to the pedestrianised zone.

U Dyou kozlu

Corner of Jostova and ul. 9. kvetna
Old town centre
🍺 *Kozel pale and dark 12*
🕐 *Daily 1100-2400*

A busy, multi-roomed, street-corner beer restaurant which gets full by mid-evening with a wide age range of customers who are only there for the beer. Its popularity, especially with students, may not be unrelated to the low prices and nearby tram junction on Brandlova. Someone should try to come up with a more original name for the place – especially if they change their brewery supplier.

Zemsky Dum

Corner of Maresova and Kounicova
Northern end of old town centre
🍺 *Staropramen pale 10, 12 and dark 10*
🕐 *Mon-Sat 1100-2300*

A long, single-roomed bar with department store display windows doesn't sound attractive, but on the inside there is a pleasant pub atmosphere. The pub caters for a broad mix of people, although in the evenings it's popular with students, drawn perhaps by the big cooked meals at student prices. The Zemsky is on a corner next to a big illuminated sign advertising a Bingo hall.

Plzenska

Vessela (behind the Hotel International)
Off Ceska pedestrianised street
🍺 *Pilsner Urquell, Gambrinus 12, Purkmistr dark, Prior wheat (bottled)*
🕐 *Daily 1100-2200*

An up-market beer restaurant with slick waiters and crisp white table cloths, but also a big and varying selection of beer from the Pilsner Urquell group.

The traditional food is of a high quality, although not expensive, and the menu (ask for an English version) offers suggestions to go with particular beers, from cold nibbles to full meals. Apart from the ubiquitous pork and dumplings, there's grilled carp and roast Moravian duck. Or you can just drink and watch the other customers eat. Not for lovers of Skupina IV.

Smichovska Pivnice

Starobrnenska, near the cathedral
🍺 *Staropramen pale and dark 10*
🕐 *Mon-Fri 0900-2300; Sat 0800-1400*

This is a no-frills traditional workers' boozer where, curiously, they turn off the taps when the shops close on Saturdays.

Skipeke U Rytire

Starobrnenska
🍺 *Cerna Hora pale and dark 12*
🕐 *Daily 1700-0200*

One of Brno's few watering holes which start late and finish late, and a rare outlet for the little state brewery 25 kms north of Brno which probably has an uncertain future. It's a cellar bar popular with Brno's trendy young, so it never gets too crowded. You'll find it tucked away in a courtyard opposite the Smichovska pub. Light meals.

Pivnice Radegast

Dominikanska, near the cathedral
🍺 *Radegast pale 10 and 12*
🕐 *Daily 1000-2200*

One of a clutch of newish bars hugging the hillside below the cathedral. Rents must be low round here. If the owners changed the beer supplier, they'd have to change the pub's name too, so it must be a long contract.

U ZLATEHO

Mecova 3

Off Dominikanske namesti

🍺 *Pilsner Urquell and Budvar 12.*

🕐 *Daily 1100-2200*

Unusual to find this pair of beers on sale together. Budvar is a rarity in Brno. A small, cheerful bar.

STATION BUFFET
(hlavni nadrazi bufet)

In the railway station

🍺 *Starobrno pale and dark 10*

🕐 *Daily 0700-2130*

The stand-up buffet offers the cheapest beer in town, and the least salubrious place to drink. Starobrno beers are hard to find beyond the brewery tap, apart from in Brno's ritziest hotels. Here, they are almost giving it away at 5.30 crowns (14 pence) a half litre. No wonder the ornate and cavernous station restaurant next door is unloved.

KE NAMESTI

🍺 *Pilsner Urquell and Budvar 12.*

🕐 *Daily 1100-2200*

Unusual to find this pair of beers on sale together.

Pegas, Brno brew pub

BREWERIES AROUND BRNO

At the beginning of 1996, seventeen breweries within an 80 km (50 miles) radius of Brno were reported to be still producing. One of them, at Boskovice near Cerna Hora, has recently re-opened after being closed since 1954. Its output is reported to include a wheat beer.

The other breweries are at: Breclav (south on the Austrian border), Brumov-Bylnice (on the Slovakian border near Uhersky Brod), Cerna Hora (featured below), Jihlava (west of Brno), Litovel (near Olomouc), Olomouc (featured below), Policka (north, near Svitavy), Prerov, Prostejov, (north-east), Svitavy (north), Uhersky Brod and Uherske Hradiste (south-east, close together near the border with Slovakia), Vystov (east) and Znojmo (south-west on the border with Austria).

Those at Litovel, Olomouc and Prerov are now part of one privatised company, Moravskoslezske pivovary a.s. (Moravian-Silesian Breweries) which consists of six breweries. The group has a brewing capacity of 1.5 million hectolitres (910,000 barrels), although it was operating well below capacity in 1995 after neighbouring Poland and Slovakia introduced trade protectionist measures which slashed beer imports. The other breweries in the group are at Hanusovice, Opava, and Vsetin, which is the smallest with 120,000 hl (73,000 barrels) and may be sold – according to the company because the local population prefer wine or hard liquor. The group produces more than twenty different beers.

BRECLAV

There's a little heard about brewery (240,000 hl; 145,000 barrels) in this small town in the castle-strewn countryside close to the Austrian border, directly south of Brno. It hit the local headlines in 1994 when production workers called a strike in protest at unpopular management decisions. In 1995 it was still state owned, producing among other beers two dark lagers, a locally popular Mazak 10 and a 12 called Special. The beers can be drunk in the Grand Hotel on the town's main square and at U Slavie (daily 1000-2200). The U koruna (The Crown) has virtually all Starobrno's beers on tap and serves excellent, low-cost Moravian food. Sun-Fri 1000-2200; Sat 0900-2000.

NEARBY

Close to the Czech-Austrian border on the E461 Brno-Vienna route, Mikulov is dominated by a large handsome baroque castle where the peace treaty ending the Austro-Prussian war was signed in 1866. The best pub in the locality is U rohaty krokodil (Horned Crocodile): Starobrno's pale 10 and 12 beers. Daily 0900-2200.

CERNA HORA

Twenty minutes north of Brno on the E461 road to Svitavy (regular buses from Brno), densely wooded gentle hills rise round an old brewery where they still turn the malt shovel. Malting barley for beer has been going on here since at least the early 1500s when records also first mention brewing. The labour-intensive Pivovar Cerna Hora in the small town of the same name not only survived the Communist centralisation and rationalisation of the Czech brewing industry, but also kept its ancient maltings in vaulted cellars despite the major maltings centre at nearby Prostejov.

In 1995, the run-down brewery had reverted back to state ownership after a buyer in 1994 failed to pay the successful bid price following the six-month grace period which accompanies some purchases from the state. But the 340 employees were bracing themselves for another privatisation and possibility of redundancies; it's hard to imagine that a private owner would retain the cavernous hand-worked maltings. The yellow-stuccoed tower brewery also still uses traditional open fermentation squares and horizontal lagering tanks, but there is a move to pasteurisation of the beer, which will eventually afflict every brand once all aluminium casks have been replaced with the dustbin-shaped keg. Up to 20 per cent raw sugar is used in all beers as well as a mix of hop extract and whole hops (Zatec and Moravian). And the recent trend has been to produce weaker beers to meet very price-sensitive local custom – hence a new pale lager called Hardy (after a local radio station) at 9 degrees (3.5 abv).

Cerna Hora's beers tend towards a malty flavour: the pale 10, called Tas, is the driest with a yeasty aroma; the Granat dark 12 – the brewery's oldest brand – is very malty with a sweetish aftertaste.

Cerna Hora's annual brewing capacity is below 200,000 litres (about 120,000 barrels), placing it in the country's "small beer" category. The brewery is operating below capacity.

In Cerna Hora, the brewery "tap" is the basic U Korcu on the main street, Brnenska. In Brno, some of Cerna's beers are at the Skipeke U Rytire, on Starobrnenska in the old town centre, and at Cernohorska Pivnice on Kapucinske namesti at the start of the old town in front of the railway station.

OLOMOUC

Deep in the Moravian countryside, this ancient ecclesiastical town has more protected historic buildings in the Czech Republic than anywhere else apart from Prague. It's one of those architectural gems of central Europe which was moth-balled for more than half a century by the political extremism which ebbed and flowed across the region. Olomouc was an important cog in the Holy Roman Empire of the middle ages. Its university was founded in 1573. It was capital of Moravia before Brno, and Austrian emperor Francis Joseph I was crowned here after the Hapsburgs discreetly fled Vienna for a time during Europe's revolutionary rumbling in the mid-nineteenth century – no doubt comforted by Olomouc's catholic Germanic credentials (German-speaking settlers from the middle ages dominated the town until Czech independence in 1918. Olomouc was known by the German name Olmutz). When the Pope thought it was worthy of an official visit in 1995, the town's brewery celebrated with a special beer called Pilgrim (Poutnik). The gastronomic thrill here is a glass of the black lager Granat, and a plate of the local pungent curd cheese called, appropriately, Olomoucke.

Pivovar Olomouc is one of a group of six breweries in the region privatised by the government to form Moravskoslezske pivovary (Moravian-Silesian Breweries, see above).

Group export manager Stanislav Jakubik said the new company's natural domestic markets faced fierce competition from the country's most successful post-Communist brewing company, Radegast. "We don't think their beers are any better than ours, but they are very profitable and put back a lot of money into promotion and marketing."

Perhaps a decision in 1995 to begin brewing the Texan mass market lager Lone Star at Olomouc is not the answer.

GETTING THERE

Express buses run frequently from Brno and take about one hour 20 minutes. Book a seat ahead if you can at Brno bus station otherwise you could end up standing. The single fare is about 55 crowns (less than £1.50). Trains meander to Olomouc from Brno. By car, it's 65 kms (40 miles) on the E462 road northeast out of Brno via

Prostejov, which is the Czech Republic's main centre for malting barley, especially roasted malt. There are breweries at Vyskov and Prostejov.

GETTING AROUND

Both bus and train stations are within walking distance of Olomouc's historic heart, which is extensive but can easily be walked around. The attractive, nineteenth-century tower structure of the Olomouc brewery is visible from the bus station (in Holice suburb).

STAYING

The national tourist agency Cedok can book rooms – ranging from the 300-bed Communist era Interhotel Flora to modest-priced private family accommodation. Their local office, which also has town maps, is in the main square: Horni namesti 2, 77200 Olomouc. tel 068-28831, fax 24431.

WHAT TO SEE

Focal point of the old centre is Horni namesti, a huge cobbled and pedestrianised square with a beautiful, fairytale-like fourteenth-century arcaded town hall in the middle, fringed by Renaissance and Baroque houses. Reflecting its prominent religious past, Olomouc is crowded out with churches and chapels and religious statues and fountains. The triple-spired St. Wenceslas Cathedral (Chram svateho Vaclava) dates from the twelfth century and stands next to the remains of Premyslid Palace, now part of the university. The last of the powerful medieval Czech dynasty, King Wenceslas III, was murdered here in 1306.

WHERE TO DRINK

Genuine traditional pubs in the centre of Olomouc have become a rarity. In the brave new world, townsfolk and visitors seem to prefer fast food cafe-bars selling Pilsner Urquell and pizza. Perhaps eventually, when the love affair with kitsch grows stale, someone will re-invent the taverns which must have existed in this ancient town once upon a time.

U HUBERTA
Corner of Denisova and Pekarni
Olomouc's Holan pale 10, served unfiltered. Granat dark (sometimes bottled only)
◓ *Daily 1000-2200*
A rare outlet for an unfiltered and unpasteurised version of the currently most popular Olomouc beer. Round the corner from St. Wenceslas Cathedral. Basic. The brewery said unfiltered beer could also be tried in the Revina, a big pub on the Lasce housing estate.

GASTRO CENTER J&R
Svobody 31
▥ *Olomouc pale 10, Granat, Radegast pale 12*
◓ *Mon-Sat 1000-2200*
A big, ugly modern eating and drinking complex befitting its unromantic name.
The Olomouc pale and dark 10 can also be drunk in the Nadrazni Restaurace at the railway station. Daily 0800-2200.

JIHLAVA

Silver not beer was once this pretty town's claim to fame. At one point in the Middle Ages, Jihlava was the chief source of silver in central Europe and coinage for the Bohemian monarchy was minted here. The discovery of silver in Kutna Hora ended Jihlava's precious metals eminence, but the prosperity of those times is reflected in the wealth of architecture in the substantially preserved old town, in particular the typical Czech elongated main "square" which is one of the biggest of its kind in the country. The composer Gustav Mahler grew up here.

The town's brewery (see Breweries chapter) recently achieved prominence – and perhaps a new lease of life, too – when it was bought by the Austrian brewing company Zwettl. Jihlava was originally founded by German settlers more than 700 years ago and was a major German-speaking centre until the ethnic cleansing of 1945-6. The German name for the town – Iglau – is believed to be linked with local folklore about a hedgehog (Igel in German) and some of the brewery's beers are today called Jezek – hedgehog.

The best place in Jihlava to drink hedgehog beers is at the brewery tap, Pivovarska Restaurace, next to the brewery on Vrchlickeho 2. As the name implies, there are good solid, moderately priced meals here too (Mon-Fri 0900-2100; Sat 0900-1400). Two other good places to sample the local beer, which are open seven days, are Restaurace Praha on Kollorova 17, and Na hlinisti, on the street of the same name.

For road travellers, Jihlava is conveniently located just off the motorway linking Brno with Prague.

PROSTEJOV

This is the centre of the Moravian malting industry and home of Pivovar Prostejov, a young brewery by Czech standards – built in 1897. The small brewery has a capacity of about 200,000 hl (121,000 barrels) but has recently been producing only about half this amount. Prostejov's traditional export markets in eastern Europe have been undermined by protectionist measures, particularly in Poland and Slovakia since it broke away from the Czech federation. The brewery uses the Jecminek trade mark after a Moravian king whose name is sometimes alternated with Gambrinus as the patron saint of Czech brewing. During 1995 the brewery began offering an unfiltered pale 12 on draught to a wide range of pubs in the district. The best place to try Prostejov's beers is at Hotel Jecminek (Mon-Sat 1000-2300; Sun 0900-2100), on the town's main square.

SLAVKOV U BRNA

The German language name for this place 20 km (12 miles) directly east of Brno just off the D1 motorway is Austerlitz, which students of Napoleonic history know was the site of a decisive and bloody battle in the French dictator's military takeover of central Europe at the beginning of the nineteenth century. The French humiliated the Russian and Austrian armies on 2 December, 1805, when more than 30,000 men died. The battle and the deaths are commemorated with a huge Art Nouveau memorial on a hill at the village of Prace outside Slavkov (signs to Mohyla Miru, the Peace Memorial). There are battle museums at Prace and at nearby Slapanice. The large Baroque Kaunitz Castle in Slavkov u Brna has a much bigger museum devoted to Napoleon and the battle. Thirsts are best quenched with beer from the Vyskov brewery at the U Nadrazi adjacent to the railway station in Slavkov u Brna (daily 1100-2200).

VYSKOV

The status of the small brewery in this little industrial town between Brno and Olomouc was uncertain in early 1996. It was linked in a government sell-off with the breweries at Cerna Hora, Jarosov and Uhersky Ostroh. The history of the Vyskov brewery reaches back to 1680 when it was built and initially operated by the catholic church under the aegis of the Bishop of Olomouc. The brewery was owned by the Olomouc diocese until 1945, although rented out to various brewing tenants.

Predictably, Vyskov has a 200 year-old castle, now a local history museum. Look for Vyskov beers in Sumavan Hotel bar (daily 1000-2300).

ZNOJMO

The small private Hostan brewery (216,000 hl, 130,000 barrels) operates in historically cramped surroundings in this picturesque walled border town which still retains a medieval-like appearance. The brewery, which takes it name from a mid-fourteenth century brewer in the town, produces pale 10, 11 and 12 with the Hostan name, plus a dark 10 with the name adopted by so many Czech brewers – Granat. The dark is made with four different malts. The best places to drink the beers are the Hotel Dukla, on Holanska 5 (daily 1000-2200) and Restaurace Club, at Rooseveltova 36 (Mon-Sat 1100-2200). The pale beers are quite dry and hoppy. The brewery organises an annual beer festival, usually in mid-May, which also features brews from other towns. And a big harvest festival with much beer drinking is held in Znojmo every October.

A few miles west along the River Dyje (the Thaya in Austria) are two magnificent castles perched on craggy hills at Bituv and Vranov. Both date from the twelfth century.

Open fermenters at Starobrno brewery

BUD BATTLE

Was it the excellence of south Bohemian beer, or simply the attraction of a short, easy-to-remember Germanic name? We'll never know for sure, but peripatetic German-American brewer Adolphus Busch's adoption of "Budweiser" in 1876 ignited a beer trade mark battle which has been fought through the world's courts for much of the twentieth century.

It is a fascinating tale, woven with the intrigues of language, nationalism, fascism, communism and "free" market capitalism.

Contrary to some misconceptions, the American brewing company which grew into the giant Anheuser-Busch did not steal the name Budweiser from the Czech brewery Budweiser Budvar. That famous brewery was not established until 1895, some thirty years after Busch's central European tours.

Busch was German-born but moved to the United States in 1857 in the big migration of Europeans to the New World seeking fame, fortune or simply an alternative to the poverty back home. Much of the United States' brewing heritage stems from this time, often started by German entrepreneurs. Then as now, German-sounding names sold beer. About the time Busch emigrated, his future father-in-law, Eberhard Anheuser, had become a shareholder in a small brewery in St. Louis, Missouri, with a most original new world name – Bavarian Brewery.

Busch became involved through marriage in the 1860s. By then he was already an importer of Czech hops and through this developed a fondness for the fashionable Bohemian spas of Carlsbad (Karlovy Vary) and Marienbad (Marianske Lazne) where he stayed on European business trips.

Whether Busch drank beer from Budweis is unknown, but he and his future business partners developed a taste for Bohemian-German place names. One of A-B's other present-day major brands is named after another Czech town – Michelob, now named Mecholupy.

At this time, the only brewery in the south Bohemian town of Budweis – much later renamed Ceske Budejovice – was the one we now know as Samson. It was founded in 1795 from an amalgamation of German-speaking citizens with ancient brewing rights. Samson was originally called by the somewhat tortuous name Budweiser Brauberichtigen burgerliches Brauhaus (Brewery of the burghers of Budweis with brewing rights) and acquired its short, sweet biblical name only in 1865.

This is where the story becomes legally complicated. Beer brewed in the town is said to have enjoyed a good reputation for centuries as far away as the royal court in Vienna, but we don't know what that beer was called (it certainly wasn't pale, bottom-fermented lager). Brewing skills might have come easily to the burghers, but settling on a name for their town seems to have been a much greater problem – no doubt confused by simmering ethnic problems which went deeper than just language. Half the town was Czech speaking, half spoke German. The Germans dominated commerce.

The only part of the town's name which appears to be original is "Bud" – ironically the term which A-B is legally entitled to use to market its Budweiser beer in some countries of mainland Europe. Over the centuries, the town's name has changed backwards and forwards variously as Budiwoyz, Budwois, Buduoyz. During the nineteenth century and until Czech independence they settled on Budweis. After independence from Austria 1918 it became Ceske Budejovice. When the British and French governments nodded approval of Nazi Germany's plan to annex parts of German-speaking Bohemia (the so-called Sudetenland) in 1938, it reverted back to Budweis. In 1945-6, the town's German-speaking population was forcibly expelled across the borders into Austria and Bavaria, and the town once again became Ceske Budejovice – which roughly means Czech Budweis.

It wasn't until 1882 that Samson registered the names Budweiser Export Lager Bier and Budweiser Burgerbrau. For a time Samson was noted for strong black beers, one of which was marketed as Porter. Some Samson beers may have been exported to the U.S. in the early 1870s, but when the Budweiser label was first used for export markets is unclear.

The brewery we now know as Budweiser Budvar was established with Czech speakers' money as part of the rising wave of Czech nationalism gnawing at the Hapsburg reins, and to counter the commercial dominance of the region by German speakers. The new Czech-speaking brewery – called Cesky akciovy pivovar – quickly became an aggressive rival to Samson. There was a local price war, then the two settled into export market competition. During this time Anheuser-Busch also began to grow.

The two Czech breweries came together in 1911 to reach a simple trade mark agreement with A-B. The two Bohemian breweries acquired the tag "Original Budweiser" and carried on exporting, and in return A-B could use its "Budweiser" name everywhere except Europe. Neither side was content with the terms, but in the meantime came World War One, Czech independence and Prohibition in the U.S. Both Bohemian breweries continued to export beers with various names: Budweiser, Budbrua, Budbrau.

It was only in 1930 that the name "Budvar" was first used – by the Czech-speaking brewery. This led in 1936 to the company we know as Budweiser Budvar changing its title to "Budvar – Cesky akciovy pivovar Ceske Budejovice". It was a minefield of confusion.

Before World War Two, Budvar produced a range of pale and dark 10 to 13 degree beers, but the name change was to help protect its increasingly popular pale lager. Let's not forget though that dark lagers were much more prominent then, and even until the early 1950s about 45 per cent of Budweiser Budvar's output was dark beer, production of which stopped only in the early 1960s.

The name change led to a successful trade mark patent in the U.S. in 1937. This allowed Budvar to market beer in the U.S. using the amazingly long-winded title "Imported Original Bohemian Budweiser Beer from Budweis City" – even though the town of origin was now officially called Ceske Budejovice.

Only one year later, German Nazi occupation forces marched into much of Bohemia, later taking over all Czech lands. This undermined the foreign activities of the Czech-owned brewery and revived the fortunes of the German-speaking Samson Brewery which had become overshadowed by Budvar. The Nazis renamed the town Budweis. After their defeat in 1945, the Samson Brewery was confiscated by the state as an "enemy" and all its trademark rights transferred to Budvar. Naturally, the town's name changed back again too.

The Communist takeover in 1948 put a block on any renewed trade mark negotiations between Ceske Budejovice and St. Louis for a number of years, until the Communists woke up to the money-spinning potential of beer exports. By then, A-B's grip on American markets and growth world-wide had grown considerably.

Today, A-B is the world's biggest brewing company, with an annual output of about 90 million hl (55 million barrels) from a dozen breweries – more than Britain's entire annual beer production and five times the Czech Republic's entire annual production of 18 million hl (11 million barrels). Given such a colossal business – which also controls more than 40 per cent of the entire U.S. beer market – it is not surprising that some people are a little suspicious of A-B's desire to buy into a brewery in the middle of the Bohemian forests which can brew little more than a spit of A-B's production. Expressed as a percentage, Budweiser Budvar's operation today is just one percent of A-B's.

The top men in St. Louis have said they are interested in helping to develop Budvar's world markets. But would Budvar be safe in A-B's hands? Is the American giant perhaps more mindful of the huge European markets still waiting to be won if the Czech Budweiser brand was out of the way? We have seen what is possible in Britain – the odd man out in Europe – where both Budweiser brands can be legally marketed in their full glory. The marketing muscle of A-B has pushed its "King of Beers" into virtually every pub in Britain, but how many sell the Czech Budweiser? With the rival Czech trade mark out of the way, the European sales potential for A-B would be big even by A-B's standards.

Trade mark negotiations resumed in 1986 and have been going on ever since. Costly trade mark litigation between the two rivals in a number of countries was suspended in 1990 for a time while the first non-Communist Czech government after the collapse of the Iron Curtain listened to A-B's overtures. The U.S. giant has talked about buying one third of Budvar. But domestic opposition to A-B has grown, encouraged by petitions and delegations from the Campaign for Real Ale urging independence. A-B was irritated with CAMRA's success in raising the international profile of the issue. The St. Louis management tried showering dollars on the Czechs – big donations to Czech educational institutions, including Ceske Budejovice University, placatory advertisements in Czech newspapers, and even taking over a smart, five-storey building in Budejovice and converting it into the "St Louis Center" to disseminate American cultural niceties. At the end of 1994, when the carrots hadn't worked, they resorted to sticks and ended the truce on world-wide court proceedings over the trade mark issue. Towards the end of 1995, it was rumoured but not substantiated that A-B intended to cut back on its big annual purchase of Czech hops – between 15 and 20 per cent of the production total – to put pressure on the Prague government.

It is hard to fathom exactly what game the Czechs are playing, or whether they are simply dithering. The men from St. Louis are not the only suitors. Brewing companies from Britain, Germany and Austria (whose brewing companies have been the most successful to date in buying into the Czech brewing industry) have made bids. Bass has expressed interest.

At the beginning of 1996, Budvar was the last major brewery still owned by the Czech state, an indication, perhaps, of the concern for the famous beer's fate. The government has sold other leading businesses – notably Pilsner Urquell – with restrictive covenants on re-sale and foreign ownership. But these restrictions are limited. In Urquell's case, for example, Czech shareholders cannot sell to foreigners for a maximum of five years. That restriction expires in June 1999.

Both sides in the Budweiser Battle know that the trade mark conflict is at the heart of the issue. In a commentary in a brewery book marking Budvar's centenary in October 1995, the anonymous author wrote: "The brewery considers its Trade Marks the most valuable spiritual asset and has always taken great care for their registration and protection."

The rumour mill surrounding the future of Budweiser Budvar has worked overtime in recent years. At one stage, the Czech government was reported to have given preferential purchasing status to A-B when privatisation comes, but if true it didn't seem to mean much in St. Louis.

In 1995, reports resurfaced that the brewery might rejoin its home town rival Samson, which is now a partner in the privatised South Bohemian Breweries (with Regent of Trebon and Platan of Protivin). This group – mainly owned by Czech banks and investment fund groups – is one of the biggest brewing companies in the Czech Republic. If Budvar became part of it, the expanded group would have a combined annual brewing capacity of almost two million hl (1.2 million barrels) – making it one of the country's top three. Some supporters of the idea, including at least one senior government minister, believe this would make Budvar less vulnerable to foreign predators.

Although Budvar and Samson are old rivals, they were linked for more than forty years during the Communist era and separated only in 1991. An illustration of the uncertainty surrounding Budvar can be gleaned in this cryptic comment from an executive at Budvar: "Any merger (with Samson) can be theoretically realised after privatisation of Budweiser Budvar."

Meanwhile, Budvar has been doing very nicely since the end of Communism without A-B's help. By the end of 1995, it had doubled beer output in six years to 900,000 hl (550,000 barrels).

If the Czech government can impose restrictive ownership covenants, why doesn't it sell Budvar? State ownership goes against the grain of Prime Minister Vaclav Klaus's Thatcherite free market principles. Or have the foreign suitors so far simply not offered enough for Budvar?

HOPS

In the days when ale in the British Isles meant something sweet and perhaps flavoured with ivy berries or the minty leaves of costmary, the foreign hop was something akin to the marijuana plant, a banned substance.

Insular island wariness resulted in the hop being outlawed by royal decree in England for more than one hundred years in the Middle Ages. It was dubbed the "wicked weed", and at one point in the fifteenth century the city of London council petitioned parliament for hops to be prohibited in ale because they "spoyl'd ye taste of ye drink and thretend ye lives of ye folk".

This hatred of hops is all the more curious given the fact that the dried flowers of the vigorous climbing plant had been used in brewing in central Europe since at least the time of Charlemagne in the early ninth century. Monastic records reveal that Bohemian hops were being traded across Europe at the beginning of the tenth century during the stable era of the Frankish empire – more than 150 years before William the Conqueror arrived in England.

Hop plants, or more likely dried hops, are believed to have found their way across the North Sea to England in the late 1300s with merchants from Hanseatic and Flemish ports. The oldest and biggest port in northern Europe then was Hamburg, which since the eleventh century had enjoyed a lively trade in hops. There was even a special hop market in the port – Forum Humuli (after the Latin name for the hop) – and many of the hops on the Hamburg market came from Bohemia via boat along the River Elbe.

What remains unclear is when hops were first used in brewing. The Romans reported, with some disgust, that the Germanic tribes drank an alcoholic beverage called ale or beer. The Roman chronicler Pliny the Elder, who travelled extensively in the north European provinces of the Roman empire, wrote about the hop in the first century as a cultivated plant which was eaten. The hop plant grew wild in mainland Europe and its soporific properties were used in herbal medicine as a sedative.

The region now called Bohemia was occupied in turn by various Germanic and Slavonic tribes but it was the seventh century before it became permanently settled by the ancestors of today's Czechs. The Slavonic Bohemians may have discovered the hop plant's benefit to brewing, although they are thought to have acquired the habit of beer drinking from neighbouring Saxon and Frankish tribes. But it may also be that evangelising monks from southern Europe introduced the hop to the brewing cauldron north of the Alps. Monasteries were the centres of knowledge and development during the Dark Ages after the Romans.

Ironically, about the time that hops were first being outlawed in English ale making, Bohemia's King Vaclav (Charles) IV – a Holy Roman Emperor – was threatening the death sentence for any Bohemian who dared to sell whole hop plants abroad. The Bohemians wanted to keep the hop growing business to themselves.

The favoured area for growing prized Bohemian hops, then as now, was in the north-west of the Czech lands. Czech hops are still known abroad by the German name for the main hop trading town of the area – Saaz. Today the town is called Zatec.

A lucky combination of soil and geography have given Bohemian hops their present-day eminence. For years they have been the most sought after and thus the most expensive because of their distinctive aromatic qualities, but this prized status could today be under threat from foreign imitators. Other hop growing countries – notably Germany and the United States, and increasingly China – produce far more hops than the Czechs but none has yet successfully matched the distinctive Saaz character, although attempts are being made in the U.S. by Anheuser-Busch and reportedly also by the Germans in Bavaria's Hallertau hop-growing district.

The threat of imitation undermining the future of the Bohemian hop industry persuaded the Czech parliament in late 1995 to introduce a new law regulating the export of Saaz hops. Crops will in future require a certificate of quality. Any which fail a quality inspection will be refused a certificate and cannot be exported. The industry hopes that this "Produced in Bohemia" tag will reassure export markets perhaps tempted to buy "Saaz" developed and grown elsewhere. The chairman of the Zatec Hop Growers' Union, Mr Frantisek Chvalovsky, supported the legislation saying Saaz hops are "really unique and need protecting".

A combination of three environmental factors help produce high-quality Czech hops so highly prized world-wide. These are iron-rich red brown soil, an average daytime temperature of 16-18C and eighteen hours of daylight in the peak growing period.

Just as most of the beer we drink today would be unrecognisable to a medieval tippler, so today's hops are different to their distant forebears. Late twentieth-century Saaz hops are derived from varieties bred in the previous century. They are known as Bohemian Red, or Red-Bine, so called after the colour of the soil in which they grow and the reddish tinge of the plant's snaking stems. They are low in acids but rich in resins which produce the distinctive aroma growers in other areas of the world have found impossible to replicate.

Similarly favourable conditions have led to hop growing in the south-west of the new Czech Republic around Olomouc in

Moravia, where some of the country's best malting barley is grown.

Unfortunately today the Czech hop industry is under the same kind of commercial pressures and threats to its traditions as the country's breweries. Czech hop production at about 10,000 tonnes a year is less than 10 per cent of the world total and the cost of increasing production is beyond many of the 300 small growers. The high prices charged to foreign buyers have provided a good income but have also pushed Czech brewers almost out of the market. Up to 85 per cent of Czech hops are exported, and for some years the American brewing giant Anheuser-Busch has been the biggest single customer, buying between 15 and 20 per cent of the annual crop.

But at the end of 1995 A-B said it was reducing its annual Czech hop purchase, worth more than £500,000 to the growers. A-B said it was developing it own fields of aromatic hops in the U.S., but reports suggested that A-B was really cutting back to put pressure on the Czech government, which for more than three years had resisted the American giant's efforts to buy into the prized Budweiser Budvar brewery (see Budweiser Battle).

Meanwhile, Czech growers are coming under pressure from domestic brewers to produce more of the cheaper bittering hops instead of the aromatic type. This might make the market more accessible to Czech brewers and less dependent on foreign buyers, but could it threaten the future of Bohemia's distinctive aromatic hops? The Czech Hop Research Institute has bred two new bittering varieties and trial commercial batches were expected to be grown during 1996.

The town of Zatec – which has its own small brewery (see Breweries and North Bohemia) – recognises its debt to the hop. Where other towns might have erected a stone monument to a favourite son or illustrious mayor, Zatec has a shrine-like miniature hop garden in front of its town hall on the main square.

The insular English may have been suspicious of the hop, but they evidently knew exactly where it came from and what it achieved. A Tudor chronicler called Madox Hueffer quoted a Kent landowner in 1520 as saying: "The Almains (Germans) called the plant hopfen, but "hop" is a good enough word for me. From Bohemia cometh this goodly vine that I am minded to plant in the county of Kent."

German beer must have been imported and enjoyed then, because the Kent man is reported to have added: "With the vine's aid is made that good drink that we call Brunswick Mum, but the Almains call it "bier" for it is made from the bere or barley plant. It is like our own ale, but not so sweet." The Czech word for hops is chmele.

BREWERIES

The 25 breweries described here in detail have been chosen from the 75 or so in the Czech Republic for several reasons, but not least because they offer the best cross sectional guide to the state of brewing in the country today. Some, like Budweiser Budvar, Pilsner Urquell and Staropramen are of great historical significance; a few, such as Radegast and Velke Popovice, represent the thrust of market developments today; some come under the microscope because they have been bought by foreign interests, e.g. Krusovice and Starobrno; others are here because, well, in five years' time they might be gone.

BRANIK

SOUTHERN PRAGUE, PART OF PRAGUE BREWERIES

Branik was a brand new brewery in the very first year of the twentieth century, and evidently aims to have a similar status for the start of the twenty-first. In pursuit of that goal, Prague's second largest brewery proudly lays claim to a dubious distinction – the first in the Czech Republic to replace traditional brewing methods with closed rocket launcher-like conical fermentation tanks. It is probably coincidence, but a wide cross-section of drinkers have since described Branik's everyday beers as "thin".

Branik embarked on a major rebuilding and modernisation programme in 1992 before Bass bought into the company. The brewery boasts a new brewhouse and a pasteurisation and kegging system to complement the conical fermenters. The developments have expanded brewing capacity to 600,000 hl (360,000 barrels). Branik still has its own maltings.

The original new Branik brewery of 1900 was called the Common Brewery of the Prague Brewers and Innkeepers, reflecting the amalgamation of about ten historic house breweries which had existed in the old town since medieval times. They joined forces in a cooperative to compete with the new, bigger industrialised breweries in Smichov and Holesovice and once production was under way in Branik most of these brewhouses closed down. Another casualty of the Branik greenfield site development was an old Dominican monastery brewery in what was then Branik village. The cooperative bought this brewery and promptly closed it.

During the Second World War many Czech-owned breweries suffered from the Nazi occupation; in Branik's case brewing was not only suspended, part of the brewery was converted into a warplane parts factory.

Branik has always been associated with dark beers and was once famous for a strong 14 degree Bavarian-style lager. Today, a seasonal pale 14 is brewed in small quantities at Christmas for several Prague pubs, including Branicky Sklipek (see Prague Pubs). Most of Branik's beer is sold within Prague, and 75 per cent of it is now 10 degree. The brewery recently re-adopted the figure of St Vaclav (Wenceslas) on its logo, which they originally used in 1900.

For many years the Czech Brewers' and Maltsters' Research Institute has had a small experimental brewery attached to Branik.

BUDWEISER BUDVAR

CESKE BUDEJOVICE, SOUTH BOHEMIA

Budvar is perceived as one of the two major brewing jewels in the Czech family silver chest. Although widely appreciated abroad for its single pale brand, Budvar has probably achieved as much fame for its David and Goliath battles with Anheuser-Busch, the world's biggest brewing conglomerate, which also produces the much bigger selling American Budweiser beer. A trademark dispute over the name "Budweiser" has been in progress through the world's courts on and off for more than half a century.

The problem has intensified since the demise of the Czech communist regime in 1989 left the Czech brewing industry more vulnerable to the pressures of external market forces. Since then, Anheuser-Busch (A-B) has been trying to buy a sizeable stake in the Budejovice firm, and few believe it is because the American company wants to help develop the Czech Budweiser. No doubt for this reason, Budweiser Budvar was the last big Czech brewery still in state ownership at the beginning of 1996. (See The Budweiser Battle for full story). But A-B has not been the only foreign suitor knocking at

Budvar's door. Since 1990, the Czech government – acting as a Victorian father – has received and rejected about 50 proposals of marriage from foreign brew companies.

Budvar has expanded enormously since 1989. By the end of 1995 beer production had doubled in six years to 900,000 hl (more than half a million barrels), with foreign markets accounting for nearly 60 percent of that. Budvar exports more beer than any other Czech brewery; almost half goes to the Germans. Britain is the second biggest importer and 27 other countries line up behind. But sadly the growing appreciation abroad is not reflected at home where the trend, as with most other beers, was for a cheaper, weaker 10 degree version of the real thing. At the beginning of 1996, 20 per cent of Budvar's production was "10" beer.

Budvar has been a fiercely proud and independent and, at times, rebel brewery since it began brewing in 1895. It was established as part of the growing Czech nationalism of the late nineteenth century. The Czechs saw themselves as the inferior of several "nations" within the Austrian Hapsburg empire. In the 1890s, the population of Budejovice was split 60-40 between Czech and German speakers, but the "Germans" ran the local economy – including brewing. The rival Samson Brewery – then known by its German name Budweiser Brauberichtigen burgerliches Brauhaus – had been founded exactly 100 years earlier in 1795 from an amalgamation of citizens holding medieval brewing rights. It must have been this brewery, and not Budvar, which inspired the

German-American businessman Adolf Busch during a tour of Europe and led to the creation of the St. Louis Budweiser beer in 1876. Or perhaps he just liked the Germanic name for Ceske Budejovice – Budweis.

Budvar was originally called the Cesky akciovy pivovar, or Czech Joint Stock Brewery. It was one of several businesses established by Czech finance to rival local German business dominance. The first beer – nothing like today's famous pale brand – was popular from the outset. The brewery's founders had installed the latest bottom-fermenting (lager) technology being created for a rapidly industrialising brewing industry. Only two years after opening, the brewery won a gold medal at an international brewing exhibition in Stuttgart, and its beers were being sold in Prague, Vienna and Trieste. By 1908 the brewery was producing 136,000 hl (83,000 barrels) a year and export markets stretched across Europe and north America. This is the same year that the brewery engaged in a price war with neighbouring Samson over domestic trading restrictions.

Twice this century, the Budvar brewery has been a victim of political meddling. First, in 1938, it fell under the control of the Nazis after Britain and France agreed to let Hitler's Germany take over large swathes of German-speaking Bohemia. The brewery suffered because it was a wholly Czech owned business, and its pursuit of world trade marks in competition with Anheuser-Busch were halted. Second, after the Nazis were defeated and the German-speaking population controversially expelled in an ethnic cleansing campaign, the brewery fell under the rigorous control of the communists who needed it to earn strong foreign currency.

The brewery did expand during the communist years and by 1989 annual production had reached 450,000 hl (275,000 barrels), of which two thirds was exported. But despite those rich foreign markets, the brewery was constantly starved of development funds while profits were hived off to support the country's central economy.

In late 1995, Budvar was still using open fermentation and classical lagering in horizontal tanks for export market beer, but the rocket-launcher style closed continuous fermentation tanks were making inroads. However, head brewer Josef Tolar expressed a preference for traditional lagering methods and there was talk of maintaining it for the export market. But the open, pitch-lined fermentation squares – which expose the new beer to oxygen and air-borne micro bacteria – are doomed. "They are not big enough for our increased production", said Tolar, somewhat nostalgically. The brewhouse of eight traditional gleaming coppers is perhaps the most spectacular sight in the Czech brewing industry.

Budvar is a 100 per cent malted barley beer made with Moravian two-row varieties, but the brewery no longer has its own maltings. Full flower hops from Zatec are used. A single yeast strain known in the Czech brewing industry as No. 2 is used (Urquell uses No. 1). The brewery now maintains its own culture laboratories.

One of the key factors which helped Budvar's beers become so popular from the outset was the marrying of the latest bottom-fermenting technology with ideal naturally-soft water discovered in an ancient underground lake. Scientists estimate that less than three per cent of this water reserve has been used after many decades' use.

Unlike most Czech breweries since 1989, the bulk of Budvar's production is still the 12 degree variety, but nearly 60 per cent of this is exported and mostly in bottle form. The 12 is fermented for 12 days. For the export market it is lagered for 60-80 days, but no more than 60 for domestic consumption. A 10 degree version for the home market is lagered for 30-40 days. All the beer is now pasteurised and all draught goes into the German black plastic kegs.

Cerna Hora

Cerna Hora, near Brno, Moravia

The surprise in the mid 1990s is that this rural brewery so close to the Moravian capital and the large Starobrno brewery has survived at all. It was nominally sold in the second half of 1994 under the government's privatisation programme, but the single purchaser failed to stump up the cash within the six-month transition period and so by the beginning of 1995 it had reverted to state ownership. Cerna Hora was expected to be slotted back into the next privatisation schedule; the 340 employees at the small brewery (140,000 hl, 85,000 barrels) were philosophical about their future. Despite claiming an antecedence going back to 1530 (when medieval records make first mention of manorial

brewing there), the existing operation was founded and built in 1896 as a brewing and maltings business. In the context of the late nineteenth-century industrialisation of brewing, Cerna Hora was a small operation, initially producing about 4,000 barrels a year.

In recent years the brewery's beers have won several awards, not least the pale 12 Cernohorsky Lezak which came first in a 1987 competition marking the centenary of the national Brewing and Malting Industry Research Institute. Today, Cerna Hora's biggest seller is Tas, a pale 10 with an abv of less than three per cent which makes it cheap for the district's extremely price sensitive drinkers. A pale 9, called Hardy after a local radio station, has been introduced to cater supposedly to a younger generation said to find the 12 degree beer too "heavy". Hardy is fermented out longer and has a higher abv than the Tas 10.

Cerna Hora is very much a traditional operation. Fermentation is in open squares, lagering in horizontal tanks for up to seven weeks. Hops are from Zatec, a mixture of whole and extract (for economy). The brewery still operates its own floor maltings which have changed little since 1896; germinating barley is turned by hand. All Cerna Hora's pale malt needs are produced in-house from two-row Moravian spring barley. All beers are 80 per cent malt and 20 per cent raw sugar.

Yeast originates from Plzen and water is the local mains supply.

The brewery still sends out beer in two-aperture aluminium casks which permit air pressure dispense and this is not pasteurised. But modern dustbin-like kegs are being introduced and what goes in these is pasteurised. Brewer Frantisek Dolezel said he believed pasteurisation changed the character of Cerna Hora's beers, but the package of kegs, pasteurisation and CO_2 pressure dispense was demanded by more and more wholesalers and retailers, although he agreed that no-one had consulted the end users - the drinkers.

CHODOVAR

CHODOVA PLANA, BETWEEN PLZEN AND CHEB

A small brewery with a big turbulent history which has defied the odds to keep brewing. It was founded in 1573 and its subsequent ownership reads like a chronicle of the region. The first owners were Chods - an ancient border tribe - then came German speakers. Later it changed hands - as so many Czech manorial breweries did - as a result of the Hussite (Protestant)-Catholic wars. In 1945, its then owner - Count Walter Berchem was accused of spying for German intelligence- and he and the brewery's mostly German-speaking employees were sent packing across the nearby Bavarian border in the ethnic cleansing of 1945-6 which cleared Germaners from the region. The brewery was burned down twice (1733 and 1861) and so only the original medieval rock cellars remain. Between 1945 and 1989 it was starved of funds but despite its dilapidated state and the communist penchant for centralisation, which did for many small rural Bohemian breweries, managed to stay in business. Chodovar's early privatised sell off in 1992 ahead of its Urquell group stablemates may well have spared it from final closure. The neighbouring Cheb brewery was deemed surplus to needs in 1995 by the privatised Pilsner Urquell Corporation, which is now a much leaner four breweries (Urquell, Gambrinus, Karlovy Vary, Domazlice).

It is now 80 per cent owned by the Plevka family, whose senior member Jiri Plevka was manager of the brewery for 30 years in the communist era and is now Chairman. Chodovar has seen some serious investment from bank borrowings - including a switch from coal to gas heating. Annual production is now about 150,000 hl (91,000 barrels). Four beers - three pale and one dark - are confusingly marketed simply as Chodovar. Until recently, pasteurisation was a dirty word and some beers is still sold in unfiltered form on demand.

The brewery still operates its own maltings.

DOMAZLICE

SOUTH-WESTERN BOHEMIA

Domazlice rivals Regent in claims to being the country's oldest brewery, although the latter's pedigree is more easily definable. Today's Domazlice brewery is enjoying revived fortunes as a producer of specialist beers within the giant Pilsner Urquell group (Plzenske Prazdroj a.s.). It brews an excellent bottle-conditioned wheat beer, Prior, and the group's chief dark lager, Purkmistr. Both are distributed nationally; Purkmistr is exported to neighbouring Germany and as far as Taiwan.

Domazlice is the smallest of the four-brewery group – reduced from five with the closure of Cheb on the German border at the beginning of 1995. The quality of the Domazlice beer has improved considerably since the economic straitjacket of the communist era, and the 12 degree version of Purkmistr must now rank as one of the Czech Republic's best dark beers. Confusingly, as with other breweries, there are 10 and 12 versions of Purkmistr. Brewing of Prior – which takes its name from a defunct Plzen brewery – began in early 1995 and Czech media reports said there was a production target for that year of up to 15,000 hl (9,100 barrels).

The other significant beer brewed at Domazlice – apart from alcohol-free and diet editions of Primus (also produced in Plzen) is a pale 10 called Radni, which may be marketed in other parts of the country. In 1995, quantities of Gambrinus pale 10 – the biggest selling beer in the country – was being carted by road tankers to Domazlice from Plzen for kegging and bottling.

Domazlice's total output for 1994 was 154,000 hl (93,500 barrels). Just under one third of this was Purkmistr.

EGGENBERG

CESKY KRUMLOV

This is another link in the former medieval monopoly in brewing held by the Rosenberg dynasty in south Bohemia. As in nearby Trebon, the Krumlov brewery – named after a family which succeeded the Rosenbergs – is in a sixteenth- century former armoury. The brewery was moved there in 1635 when the castle which towers over the town was being extended and modernised. Eggenberg has been privately owned since 1991; two Czechs are the chief shareholders.

There are four beers: a pale 12, pale and dark 10 and a pale lower alcohol diet beer. Since the political change in 1989, the pale 10 has become the biggest seller and accounts for 80 per cent of output. Open fermentation is still practised in 22 squares, but the ubiquitous CK tanks have arrived here. The conical fermenters are used to produce the main pale 10 beer. On average, the enclosed conicals process lasts 17 days. Since 1993, Eggenberg has been cultivating its own single cell yeast strain, which originally comes from Budvar.

Classical fermentation takes 10-12 days, followed by classical lagering up to seven weeks (for the pale 12). Naturally-soft water which has percolated through sandstone comes from the brewery's own well. Hops are 70 per cent extract, the rest pellets, from Zatec. The malt is six-row Moravian, and three varieties are used for the dark beer.

Brewery director Rostislav Zagora says Eggenberg's beers are sold unpasteurised on draught. "They taste better without pasteurisation and there is a guaranteed shelf life of one month." Bottled versions are pasteurised.

Eggenberg is one of the few Czech breweries to actually own a pub – a cavernous hall adjoining the brewery (see Cesky Krumlov, Where to drink).

The brewery's annual capacity, since the arrival of the conical fermenters, is 200,000 hl (120,000 barrels). Most beer is distributed in Bohemia, but since 1994 there are small markets in Italy, Croatia and South Africa.

Brewery visits are only by special arrangement. Pivovar Eggenberg, Latran 27, 38101 Cesky Krumlov. Fax: 0042-337-3609.

GAMBRINUS

PLZEN, BOHEMIA

It lives permanently in the shadow of its infinitely more famous neighbour and today's partner, Pilsner Urquell, and yet this brewery which dares to name itself after the European patron saint of brewing produces the Czech Republic's biggest-selling beer brand – Gambrinus. The distinction may not last for long however. Radegast pursues closely behind.

Gambrinus has always been a big brewery; it was established in the mid nineteenth-century by a group of local businessmen – including Emil Skoda of car making fame – who were envious of the soaraway success of Urquell. And like all big breweries, in its aggressive pursuit of markets Gambrinus helped kill off several Plzen breweries along the way.

Gambrinus was originally a German community business with the name Erste Pilsner Actienbrauerei. It began brewing at the end of 1870 and by 1900 was one of Bohemia's three biggest breweries. For a long time, its most famous beer bore a name similar to its main rival – Pilsner Kaiserquell.

The name Gambrinus was introduced when the word Kaiser became unpopular after the demise of both the Austro-Hungarian and German monarchies in 1919.

A trade war with Urquell between the two world wars helped see off four other local breweries through takeover or merger, including one called Prior after which today's Urquell Corporation names its new wheat beer. By the start of the Second World War, Gambrinus was producing 330,00 hl (200,000 barrels) a year.

The communist era between 1948-89 merged Gambrinus and Urquell in a giant multiple called West Bohemian Breweries, of which these two plus Karlovy Vary and Domazlice make up today's privatised Pilsner Urquell Corporation – now the biggest Czech brewing group producing more than 3.4 million hl (about 2.1 million barrels). Gambrinus produces just over one million barrels of this total.

The race for quantity production at Gambrinus has jettisoned all traces of the famed classical Czech brewing traditions. The brewery, which stands next to Urquell, is a forest of 40 conical fermenters each holding 3,000 hl (1,800 barrels). The bulk of production is pale 10, which in the immediate post-communist era has become the "people's beer" – liquid fast food. Some pale Gambrinus 12 is also produced, plus a new (1994) pale discount beer called Primus. In summer 1995, Gambrinus became the proud owner of the biggest kegging line in the Czech Republic – handling 1,000 kegs an hour

Gambrinus uses Zatec hops, in various forms, plus Moravian barley, and has its own maltings. The locally naturally-soft water is drawn from artesian wells; whether this is the same source as Urquell remains unclear.

The brewery's former talent for brewing quality dark lagers

has been forsaken; this speciality has been taken over by Domazlice which although 57 km (36 miles) away also helps out with the kegging and bottling of Gambrinus 10 to maintain output.

More than 200,000 hl (120,000 barrels) of Gambrinus 12 is exported, some of it curiously under the German names Wenzelsbrau and Weltbrau.

HEROLD

BREZNICE, SOUTH OF PRAGUE, BETWEEN PLZEN AND CESKE BUDEJOVICE

Some Czech breweries had the death sentence hanging over them until the Velvet Revolution saved them, but this one was actually closed in 1988 in communist ratonalisation plans. The dilapidated ornate baroque buildings, dating from 1720 and part of the renovated castle next door, were scheduled to be demolished that year but brewer Stanislav Janostik persuaded the authorities to stay the execution. "I don't know why really. The situation looked hopeless. We were not to know that the dramatic political changes were just around the corner, but I just didn't want to see the buildings destroyed."

Mr Janostik, one of the most innovative brewers in the country, managed to get the brewery re-opened again in 1990, and made it the first place in the Czech lands to brew wheat beer 75 years.

In the privatisation programmes that followed, Breznice brewery was bought as part of a parcel which included the Brewing Research Institute in Prague. Some of the owners are the country's big brewers

but the situation was likely to change in early 1996. Hopefully, a single owner will be found for the brewery.

Herold is a small classical brewery producing less than 60,000 hl (36,500 barrels). Since re-opening it has been innovative, producing not only a bottle conditioned wheat beer but also a new full bodied dark beer. It may have found a niche market by acting as a contract brewer for pub distributors – the dark beer was brewed initially for a German customer who wanted something similar to the black homebrew of U Fleku in Prague. An experimental strong pale beer was being brewed in mid 1995, but sales of the wheat beer were struggling. Standard pale 10 and 12 beers are also produced. Not surprisingly, the biggest seller is the pale 10.

The brewery has its own on-site maltings, where they also produce their own wheat malt. Naturally-soft water comes from a 100-year-old well and is untreated. Hops in extract and pellet form come from Germany, Belgium and Zatec. The brewery uses 16 open fermentation squares and classical lagering is in deep natural cellars dug into the rock beneath the brewery where the temperature is steady at 2C. The beer range is matured for longer than some other Czech beers: two to three months. Draught beer for the domestic market is not pasteurised. The brewery has a policy of remaining traditional and will not switch to closed conical fermenters, said Janostik. Before producing the Herold wheat beer, he spent time with a south Bavarian wheat beer brewer to learn techniques. But, he says, his methods are different to those commonly used in Bavaria. "After all, this is Czech wheat beer, not Bavarian", he smiled. (See Tasting – Herold). Herold Wheat is produced with a top fermenting yeast from Bavaria. It is warm conditioned for one month in horizontal lagering tanks.

JIHLAVA

SOUTH MORAVIA

The 130-year-old "hedgehog" brewery survived two world wars, Nazi occupation control and communist state confiscation only to be bought by a foreign interloper in 1995 for a song – but not by a big brewing group. The new owner with a two-thirds shareholding is the comparatively small private brewery Zwettl, from just 50 km (31 miles) across the border in the Austrian market town of the same name.

Zwettl is barely bigger than Jihlava, but infinitely richer and more aggressive. It is determined to push its Zwettler beers into greater Prague and the spare capacity in Jihlava looks set to become the launching pad. Zwettl is known to have bought the cash-short Czech brewery cheaply – for an undisclosed sum – and is investing about £3 million in its modernisation and expansion.

The brewery was built in the 1860s when four German-speaking small brewers and maltsters in the town pooled their resources. The former German name for the town is Iglau. Igel in German means hedgehog and the spiky creature is part of the town's emblem and is said to have ancient fairytale connections – hence several of Jihlava's beer brands are called Jezek – hedgehog in Czech.

The brewery was threatened with closure after the Second World War because of its Germanic associations, but it survived and expanded and prospered in the 1950s and 1960s because of the communist state's closure of several nearby smaller breweries.

The brewery has been remorselessly losing its classical brewing techniques. By early 1996 open fermentation squares and cellar lagering had been 80 percent replaced with closed conical tanks. In 1994 Jihlava still had it own maltings, but by the end of 1995 these had gone. Water is still drawn from two wells. The Jezek pale 11 is sometimes available locally unfiltered.

At the beginning of 1995 Jihlava was operating at only 50 per cent of its capacity. This spare capacity will have been one of the main attractions to the new Austrian owners and it will be expanded. Since 1994, Zwettl has been exporting beer into the Czech Republic made with duty-free imports of Czech raw materials under a cross-border trading deal between the two countries. As they moved in, the Austrians said with a straight face that they did not plan to brew Zwettler in Jihlava. Ho, ho. Whither the hedgehog?

KARLOVY VARY

This brewery was established in the late nineteenth century as the industrialisation of brewing gathered pace. Originally, water from the local health spa springs was used for brewing Carlsbad Mineral Beer but this practice stopped in the early twentieth century. An attempt in 1991 to use mineral water again, producing a brand called Dr Bier, failed to excite local taste buds and it has been discontinued. Until 1945 the brewery was called Brauerei Weber and the beer was Weber Brau – reflecting the fact that the local population was largely German speaking. In the post-war ethnic cleansing they were forced across the Bavarian border at gunpoint, and the beer's name was changed to Karlovarske pivo specialni (Karlovy Vary Special Beer). The biggest brand produced at Karlovy today is Karel IV, a pale 11 named after the Czech king who popular legend credits with discovering the bubbling springs which put the town on the map. During the communist nationalised years, the brewery was closely linked with its former rival in Cheb. Both breweries became part of the privatised Pilsener Urquell Corporation and in early 1995 Cheb was closed and its brands transferred to Karlovy. Today, Karlovy produces the former Cheb pale lager Wallenstein 11 (named after a seventeenth-century rebel Czech army general who was assassinated in Cheb by Irish mercenaries during the Thirty Years' War) and contributes towards production of the Urquell Corporation's mushrooming cheap pale lager brand Primus 10, which is also brewed at Gambrinus in Plzen. Total production of Primus reached almost 1 million hl in 1994 but in 1995 there were quality control problems, possibly linked to it being brewed in more than one place. It's unclear what has become of Wallenstein 12, Starovar 11 (previously brewed in Cheb), and a Karlovy Vary dark lager called Lord. In 1995, Karlovy Vary reported an annual total production of 200,000 hl (121,000 barrels).

KRUSOVICE

RAKOVNIK

This is the bigger but more rural of two breweries adjacent to the town of Rakovnik, 50 km (31 miles) west of Prague.

Krusovice is steeped in history but despite wrapping itself in a marketing cloak of "tradition", the brewery is now a high tech stainless steel factory not unlike the larger German breweries.

Its roots are traceable back to the early sixteenth-century when it was built by the royal tax collector. The canny collector then sold it to Bohemian king Rudolf II and it became part of the royal summer hunting estate at nearby Krivoklat, where one of Bohemia's oldest fortified castles is to be found today. War debts later forced the monarchy to sell.

Since 1994 Krusovice has been 51 per cent owned by the giant German brewing group Binding and under the Germans' marketing tutelage it has given itself the grandiose title Kralovsky Pivovar Krusovice – Royal Brewery Krusovice plc. German money is now also financing a massive expansion programme with the ultimate aim of putting the brewery in the national big league competing with Pilsner Urquell to the left and Staropramen to the right.

In 1993, Krusovice brewed about 250,000 hl (151,00 barrels). By late 1995 brewing capacity had doubled to half a million hectolitres and the goal is to reach one million (over 600,000 barrels).

Backed by Binding, this rural brewery surrounded by forests and hop fields has taken the high tech road. It was the first in

Bohemia to convert 100 per cent to pressurised kegs; there is a new stainless steel computerised brewhouse – with a second one planned – a forest of conical fermenters, and pasteurisation. The brewery intends to concentrate on two or three brands because in the words of general manager Vaclav Kloub seasonal or speciality beers "do not have any great impact on the economy of the brewery".

The chairman of Binding and a member of the Krusovice board, Mr Klaus Ebrich, said during a visit to the brewery in 1995: "The market is a duel of ideas, quality and demand. Obviously there will be breweries that succumb. It would be illogical if all were to succeed." Mr Ebrich is a former banker turned marketing manager. Capturing a major slice of the Prague market is clearly part of the strategy and with neighbouring Germany saturated in beer, Binding sees the Czech domestic market as the main target for growth.

The brewery logo of a musketeer is said to be linked to the plundering of the brewery by foreign mercenary soldiers in the 1630s during the Thirty Years War.

LOBKOWICZ

VYSOKY CHLUMEC, SOUTHERN BOHEMIA

Apart from the communist era (1948-89) this small country brewery has belonged to the Lobkowicz family for at least four centuries, and is one of the oldest in the country. A pity then that its newly regained independence following restitution to the family in 1992 is spoilt by a business link-up with the giant Austrian brewers Brau AG.

Records for the Lobkowicz brewery go back to the early 1600s although the family bought the still-forested estate in 1474.

In 1995 it was still a classical Czech brewery with open fermentation and cellar lagering, although pasteurisation had been introduced and pressurised kegs had replaced traditional casks. Water comes from wells sunk beneath the estate forests. Lobkowicz also has its own maltings and produces a surplus which it sells.

The brewery produces pale 10 and 12 beers plus, unusually, a dark 12 (made with three malts) and an occasional pale 14 Special at 5.5 percent abv. The pale 12 is exported to Britain as Lobkov Export.

In return for a low interest loan of about £650,000 (26 million crowns), the Lobkowicz brewery is now producing one of Austria's biggest brands – Kaiser. The 1995 deal means that the Bohemian brewery will eventually devote up to one third of its 120,000 hl (73,000 barrel) capacity to Kaiser Premium (5 per cent abv) production. Lobkowicz expected to be producing 20,000 hl (12,000 barrels) by 1997. The agreement, which will operate for ten years, came after months of negotiations; the Lobkowicz family didn't want to sell any of its shares to Brau AG.

The Lobkowicz-brewed Kaiser will go some way towards meeting Czech tastes but will also retain some of its Austrian characteristics – lighter colour and flavour, higher carbonation – said commercial director Frantisek Cermak.

Given the cheaper labour and production costs available to Brau AG in central Bohemian town of Vysoky Chlumec, it's curious that they intend to put a premium price on Kaiser to compete with Czech national brands like Pilsner Urquell.

Lobkowiczy beers are generally distributed in central Bohemia and in Prague. It is clear that Brau AG is using Lobkowicz brewery as launch pad for Kaiser into the Prague market, which is only 75 km (47 miles) away. Brau AG has a controlling interest in the large Starobrno brewery in the country's second largest city, Brno

The full production range from Lobkowicz, including the Kaiser, can be drunk at U Hynku in Prague Old Town (see Prague Pubs). The brewery can be visited by arrangement.

MESTAN OR HOLESOVICE

PRAGUE, PART OF PRAGUE BREWERIES GROUP

The smallest of Prague Breweries' three is sometimes called by the name of the suburb – Holesovice – in which it stands on the bulbous bend of the River Vltava just north of Prague Castle. But it is more popularly known as Mestansky Pivovar – burghers' or citizens brewery. Its dark beer bears the name Mestan. Many Czech breweries built in the nineteenth century used the term mestansky as a way of defining them from the older aristocratic breweries whose powerful feudal estate owners had controlled most brewing before the industrial revolution.

Brewing began in 1897 and three years later it was producing 70,000 barrels a year.

Today's brewery is a mix of old and new - open fermentation squares, traditional lagering tanks, and a new kegging system. The brewery is perhaps most noted for its dark beer, which has won several prizes in recent years, notably at the 1995 PIVEX brewing trade fair in Brno. Mestan dark is one of the biggest selling dark lagers in the country and is popular with women. It is also being sold in cans which is still a fairly uncommon form of packaging. Four different malts are used, as well as some sugar. The brewery still produces 50 per cent of its own malt.

Some Staropramen pale 10 is brewed at this brewery. A low strength 8 degree pale beer is made for sale in factories. The pale 12 is marketed as Pragovar.

NACHOD

NORTHEAST BOHEMIA

Although before 1989 the "people" technically owned all Czech breweries, the townsfolk of Nachod have been given back their community brewery under the post communism restitution laws.

Many Czech breweries built during the mid-late nineteenth Century industrialisation of brewing were created by public subscription. Nachod's Primator Brewery (1874) was no exception but instead of becoming a private company like most, it remained owned by the town until the communist nationalisation of the industry in the late 1940s.

The brewery has been extensively modernised recently. Open fermentation was still being practised in the mid 1990s, but there was talk of introducing conical tanks to increase capacity beyond the 200,000 hl (121,000 barrels).

The brewery's private well water is said to be so pure that mothers buy it for their babies. In 1995, brewhouse experiments were under way to produce a top fermenting wheat beer.

Nachod produces crisp, dry beers: a pale and dark brown 12 and a pale 10 all under the Primator label. Caramel extract is used with the dark which has a notable coffeeish taste and very dry finish.

"The townspeople are proud to have their own brewery again", says Milan Nosek the marketing manager. Let's hope they can keep hold of it.

OLOMOUC

MORAVIA, NORTH OF BRNO

Olomouc Brewery is the sole survivor of three late nineteenth-century town breweries. It was shut by the Nazi occupiers in World War Two, but given a new lease of life when the communists took over the country in 1948.

The brewhouse was rebuilt in 1972 and annual capacity has gradually increased to about 200,000 hectolitres (121,000 barrels). Three regular beers are produced: Holan pale 10 (3.5 abv), Vaclav pale 12 (5.6) and Granat dark 12. The most popular of the three – because it's the cheapest – is Holan, but the largely unsung hero of the brewhouse is the Granat, which is sadly more popular in Taiwan where some of it is exported than in its home town. Granat is full bodied with an abv of 5.6, a rich roast malt aroma and a malty-dry flavour with a dry aftertaste. The pale beers are quite hoppy and dry. Several outlets sell Holan unfiltered at the request of their customers (see Pubs). In this form, the beer has a yeasty aroma with a much hoppier taste and a long dry finish. Worth seeking out.

Olomouc has its own on-site maltings and produces pale malt using only Moravian barley; some of the malt produced is used by other breweries in the Moravian-Silesian Breweries group. The brewery uses its own well water which is medium hard and isn't treated. Moravian as well as Zatec hops go in the brewhouse's five coppers, plus Bavarian Hallertau hop extract. Olomouc converted to closed computer-controlled fermentation in 1990 but has stayed with traditional horizontal lagering tanks – although they have quite short lagering times: 25 days for the 10 beer and 35-40 for the 12. The brewery was equivocal about pasteurisation; some beer is and wholesalers put the brewers under pressure to pasteurise it all. "It's effect on taste is negative", said an under brewer. "When we drink our beer in the brewery it is unpasteurised."

Olomouc's Chief brewer Milan Stejskal says local beer drinkers have moods of fancy, sometimes they prefer unfiltered pale beer, sometimes the trend is for Granat. Lucky people if they can dictate to the brewhouse, but within the Moravian-Silesian Breweries company there seemed a lack of commitment to Granat, which wasn't one of their main brands and was "only" ten per cent of Olomouc's output. In this first flush of post-communist enterprise, everybody wants to have a best-selling pale lager.

In late 1995, Olomouc signed an agreement with the big American brewers Heilemann to start producing that most unforgettable Texan brand, Lone Star. Presumably it's intended for drinking at Czech pub Country music nights – and don't laugh, it's a trend in Prague.

PILSNER URQUELL

PLZEN

A brewery with a profile higher than Mount Everest, but which in the last few years has lost virtually all its time-served originality and charm. In place of the unique fermenting and lagering methods used since the brewery's foundation in 1842, which survived even under the communist penchant for uniformity, there is now gleaming stainless steel and high technology. Gone are the oak fermenting vessels and the giant wooden maturation barrels which were rolled in and out of the labyrinthine cellars by hand. All that has been replaced by 104 closed conical fermentation tanks – some of which stand as tall as space Shuttle launchers and hold 3,300 hl (2000 barrels) – in a huge red metal oblong building. Production time for Urquell 12 from the brew kettle to the keg and bottle has been cut from up to eight weeks under the old system to about four weeks today.

It was widely considered that the unique environment in the damp, chilly cellars dug into the sandstone beneath the brewery and the town were an integral element in the creation of Pilsner Urquell at the open fermentation stage. An official communist handbook published in 1986 about the town of Plzen proudly proclaimed: "Since the last century beer has been produced by means of a single unchanging technological procedure. The inimitable (sic)

taste and aroma are attributed to the quality of water , the malt itself and to the microclimatic conditions of the 9km (5.5 miles) long underground corridors."

At its demise, the Urquell system – once standard in Bohemia – was as unique in the brewing world as the Burton Unions of Marston's in England.

In his Channel Four documentary on Pilsner Urquell, beer writer Michael Jackson urged the company to retain its admittedly expensive and time-consuming processes, using the comparison that people who buy vintage wine didn't expect to pay blended plonk prices. But the Urquell management evidently preferred the commercial attractions of hugely expanded markets, and the changes were approved and set in motion some time before privatisation in 1994.

The company insists that exhaustive tasting tests were carried out with panels of ex brewers and local regular Urquell tipplers to match the beer brewed by the old methods with that of the new. Corporation spokesman Jaroslav Pomp said that eventually, in blindfold tests, they all chose the beer produced in the stainless steel conical fermenters as the best. The old system was then discarded completely and parts of the fermentation and lagering cellars were earmarked for conversion into a car park. But then the company – indicating, perhaps, a little nervousness with the new high tech – announced that it intended to re-introduce the old brewing system on a small scale to allow continuous matching.

The temptation must be great, but in 1995 the company was

adamant that it would not allow Pilsner Urquell to be brewed under licence outside Plzen. "It's not possible if we want to retain the original Pilsner Urquell taste", said spokesman Pomp. Sadly, such noble beliefs haven't stopped the owners of other fine beers from going down that route. It is to be hoped that Urquell never goes that way, although there were reports in late 1994 in the Czech beer newspaper Pivni Kuryr that the Corporation had considered granting limiting foreign brewing licences.

Urquell may have lost its very special method of production – once used by all Czech brewers – but its combination of very soft well water low in salts, its own maltings using only Moravian barley, Zatec hops and a house yeast still results in a beer of distinctive quality, if arguably not the same complexity.

The Urquell Corporation's expansion since the arrival of a free market economy has been meteoric. Between 1990 and the beginning of 1995, combined production (mainly Urquell and its big sister Gambrinus next door) expanded by about 800,000 hl (490,000 barrels) to 3.3 millon hl (2 million barrels.

Today, the Urquell brewery produces 1,125,000 hl (685,000 barrels) About one third is exported to more than 50 countries. Nearly 50 per cent of Urquell's total production is bottled or canned. The biggest foreign markets are Germany and the United States.

Modernisation and investment in new technology at Urquell alone up to the beginning of 1995 is believed to have cost about £50 million. Other brewing concerns in the Czech Republic have wondered,

perhaps enviously, where that kind of money in a poor country has come from. But more big money has followed. In late 1995, Urquell negotiated a £40 million loan from the International Finance Corporation, which is an agency of the World Bank, to maintain the group's modernisation programme and reschedule short term liabilities. Part of this massive loan was covered by issuing bonds to the lenders – some of whom are German banks. It was the first IFC loan given to a private Czech business. The Urquell Corporation's owners are all Czech, a mix of big investment groups and small shareholders (holding about 10 per cent). They are barred by a government moratorium from selling – except to one another – for five years. The moratorium ends in June 1999.

PLATAN

PROTIVIN, SOUTH BOHEMIA
Records of brewing in this rural Bohemian town stretch back to the mid 1500s. Until the communist takeover in 1948, brewhouses here were always associated with aristocratic landowners. The present brewery was built in the late nineteenth century by the German-speaking Schwarzenberg family, once the biggest landowners in Bohemia. It is set in parkland surrounded by plane (platan) trees from which the brewery's beers take their name.

Through the Schwarzenberg connection Protivin beers were distributed throughout the Austro-Hungarian Hapsburg empire and many German cities such as Hamburg, Frankfurt and Berlin. Leading brewers and brewing scientists of the late nineteenth and early twentieth centuries worked at the brewery at various times, including Bohus Svoboda who set up the first Czech beer yeast propagation laboratory. But in the brewing world Protivin is most noted for its experimentation in the early 1900s with a Swiss invention for speeding up lagering times.

The Nathan System, designed by Dr. Leopold Nathan of Zurich, involved conical secondary fermenters – not unlike the high tech systems now coming into general use by lager brewers across Europe. However, Nathan-brewed beers gave off an aroma which drinkers rejected and although trials persisted the system was eventually abandoned. Under Nathan's system, beers were lagered for only two weeks instead of the normal five or six weeks.

Today, the brewery in Protivin has expanded to 350,000 hl (210,000 barrels) annual capacity and is part of the three-brewery South Bohemian Breweries group which includes Samson of Ceske Budejovice. Conical fermenters returned in 1991 under a modernisation programme which resulted in all beers being pasteurised and sent out in pressurised kegs. Moravian barley malt is used and a mixture of hop extract, and Zatec and German pelleted hops. The brewery has its own well water supply and a new one is planned.

RADEGAST

NOSOVICE DISTRICT OF FRYDEK-MISTEK, NORTH MORAVIA

The history of this burgeoning brewery is short, and as far as it is concerned sweet. For other Czech brewing companies, however, Radegast is as menacing as the pagan Slavic god after which it is named. A merger with another brewery in late 1995 took it into second place in brewing size behind the Pilsener Urquell Corporation, knocking Prague Breweries into third.

Radegast was built in the late 1960s by the communists, which was a curious move given the brewing capacity already in existence in the country, even if much of that capacity was dilapidated.

The greenfield Moravian site in the Frydek-Mistek district close to the Slovak and Polish borders seems odd now that those two countries have set up tough trade protection barriers, but in 1970 no-one could have imagined the political upheaval of 1989. The site is said to have been chosen because of excellent underground water supplies – but no doubt the proximity to the markets of the then fraternal east European Comecon countries must been an equally important factor.

Whatever the reason, Radegast was the first new brewery to be built in what was then Czechoslovakia since the early twentieth-century, making it an easy sale under the privatisation hammer after 1989. Since then, it has expanded aggressively. Unless the company overstretches itself and is forced to bring in foreign partners, which seems unlikely, it could well be the only wholly Czech-owned brewing company in the country's top five league by the turn of the century.

Radegast was already a big brewery under communist state ownership, and in 1991 it produced 1,178,00 hl (716,000 barrels). By the end of 1994, annual production was up to 1.6 million hl with further expansion up to two million hl (1,215,000 barrels) envisaged.

Because Radegast was relatively modern, it got off to a flying start when the free market replaced the communists' controlled economy. There was no trouble finding investors and today's 100 per cent Czech ownership is a mix of banks, shareholding funds and about 15,000 small investors who were allowed to take part in a so-called coupon privatisation gold rush.

Radegast was able to push out a lot of beer and capture new markets quickly while other, less modern breweries struggled to cope with the political and economic changes. Its pale 10 and 12 beers are on sale in every corner of the country. Radegast is very profitable and cash rich and according to industry sources made 130 million crowns (£3.25 million) in beer sales in 1994, a large profit in current Czech brewing industry terms. Every other Czech brewer watches Radegast closely.

In late 1995 its takeover of the Sedlec brewery in the north Bohemian town of Most, in which it had a controlling share, was completed when the debt-ridden Bohemian company was renamed Radegast Sedlec. The Most brewery – also communist-era built – was operating well under its 600,000 hl capacity, even though it had been producing some Radegast beer – notably the dark 10 – as well as its own brands since 1994. Most is much better placed for the lucrative Prague market than Radegast's home base 340 km (212 miles) to the east, and its spare capacity seems certain to

be used to produce more Radegast beers, probably at the expense of Most's three beers. Just south of Prague, Radegast has an influential 13 per cent stake in the equally popular Velke Popovice brewery, which has entered a trading partnership with the Moravian giant.

At the end of 1995, Radegast produced a strong 18 degree Christmas beer. The company indicated it could become a year-round beer.

REGENT

TREBON

This may well be the oldest continuously operating brewery in the country; it is certainly the prettiest and one of the most well cared for. Many Czech breweries have their roots in the nineteenth century industrialisation of brewing, although they might claim an establishment date reaching into the mists of time. What they often mean is that records show that someone was brewing in a particular town or locality in 1066 or thereabouts. But in Regent's case, today's brewery has been in operation in the same buildings – a converted manorial armoury – since 1698. The brewery was moved into the armoury from another town site where earlier lords of the manor (the Rosenbergs) had brewed since 1379.

Today's Regent Brewery remains a very traditional operation behind its renaissance facade. Although it is part of a private, Czech-owned group which includes Samson in neighbouring Ceske Budejovice and Platan of Protivin, Regent has its own floor maltings, producing one third of the brewery's annual pale malt needs from two-row barley grown in the locality. Outside malt, including the three other types needed for Bohemia Regent dark, comes from Moravia. The brewery's own malt is still partially turned by hand in sixteenth-century cellars.

Trebon's beers are still fermented in open squares – 47 of them – and lagered traditionally in horizontal tanks. But this is a brewery experiencing growing demand and hovering over the classic scene is the temptation to switch to continuous conical fermenters to increase production and save time. Head brewer Ivan Dufek, who is rightly proud of his beers, remains unsure: "I am a little sceptical. I think quality is best managed in small quantities. When something is too big then each mistake can have a bigger significance overall."

Trebon's 12 degree beers are allowed to ferment for ten days, using an old established house yeast whose parentage is Budvar. Naturally very soft water comes from two 300-foot deep wells sunk near the brewery in 1990. The 12 degree beers are lagered for six weeks for the domestic market and eight weeks for export, the weaker beers less. All the beers are flash pasteurised.

Today at Trebon, as elsewhere, the biggest selling beer is the pale 10. Only about 20 per cent of production is of 12 degree beer. "It is not a question of popularity, but of money. Everyone has a limited pocket", said Mr Dufek. Perhaps saddest of all is the revelation that Trebon's "famous" dark beer – marketed in Britain as Black

Regent – accounts for only two per cent of the annual 350,000 hl (210,000 barrels) output.

During the nineteenth century, under the influential aristocratic Schwarzenberg ownership – which lasted until 1945 – Trebon's dark beers were in great demand in Vienna, even at the Hapsburg court. The brewery produced porter-like 13 and 14 degree beers which were last produced in the 1920s. The only popular demand for dark beer nowadays is at Christmas time when Bohemians maintain the culinary tradition of accompanying their carp in dark sweet sauce with dark beer. The brewery takes its name from the sixteenth-century Rosenberg who set about draining the surrounding swamp lands to create the system of lakes and ponds which spawned the carp-fishing industry. Regent's trade mark is the five-petalled rose which was the Rosenberg family emblem.

Regent's beers are exported to Austria, Britain, Finland, Germany, Italy and Sweden.

Tours of the Trebon brewery are possible; there is even a visitors sampling cellar. But try to book well in advance of a proposed visit. Write to: Pivovar Regent, Trocnovske namesti 124, 37914 Trebon, Czech Republic. Regent's head brewer, Mr Ivan Dufek, speaks English. Fax (from UK): 0042-333-3385

SAMSON

CESKE BUDEJOVICE
The oldest of the two breweries in this famous brewing town known to the world as Budweis is also now the smallest and least known. Samson was founded exactly 100 years before the arrival of its arch rival,

Budweiser Budvar, and was one of the first amalgamations in the country of small brewpub owners with medieval brewing rights.

There has always been an uneasy relationship between Budejovice's two breweries; the rivalry began with the creation of Budweiser Budvar as a conscious act of nationalism by Czech speakers in 1895 because the Samson brewery – and much of the rest of the town's commerce – was dominated by German speaking citizens (until 1945-6 when ethnic cleansing rid the region of German speakers, much of Bohemia had been bilingual for many centuries).

In the very early days of the conflict with the American Budweiser producers Anheuser-Busch, Samson also produced and trademarked brands (1882) with the name "Budweiser". These trademarks, together with use of the town's crest on labelling, later went to the Budvar brewery. Samson's fortunes rose slightly over Budvar during nazi Germany's World War Two occupation, but at the end of the war Samson was confiscated by the state as "enemy" property.

Ironically, the two breweries were part of the same state-owned grouping during the communist years and only separated in 1993. Samson is now part of the privatised South Bohemian Breweries company which includes Regent of Trebon and Platan of Protivin. In 1995 they produced more than one million hl (625,000 barrels) putting them in the country's top five brewing companies. The state retains a five per cent shareholding but the bulk of shares are held by Czech banks.

During 1995 some government ministers and Samson executives proposed that the Budvar brewery should join South Bohemian Breweries as a way of protecting Budvar from foreign predators.

In 1995 Samson was still very much a classical lager brewery with a traditional brewhouse, open fermentation and lagering cellars. But, like many others, the pursuit of bigger production threatens these systems; there are plans for conical continuous fermenter tanks. And most beer is now pasteurised. Output in 1994 was 325,000 hl (200,000 barrels) and the aim is for 500,000 hl.

Years ago Samson was noted for strong dark lagers, including a Porter 20 degree, but these faded away, and whether it was because of raw material shortages in communist times or the alleged tidal demand for pale beer is forgotten. However, in line with some other breweries, Samson re-introduced a dark 10 beer in 1993, although it is still only a very small percentage of production. Nearly 80 per cent of production is currently pale 10, reflecting the domestic swing to weaker, cheaper beers; about 11 per cent is pale 12. Whole hops from Zatec are used only for the 11 and 12 beers; the "people's" 10 degree beers get hop pellets and extract. The 12 degree beer is still lagered for eight weeks; 10 gets three weeks.

The brewery still has its own floor maltings which provide 60 per cent of brewhouse needs, although specialist dark malts are bought in.

A darker coloured and slightly more bitter version of Samson's pale 11 beer is produced for Britain's Wolverhampton and

Dudley brewery who market it as Zamek. The pale 12 is exported to the U.S. as Crystal and the dark 10 as Diplomat Dark.

The brewery acquired the name Samson (linked to the statue of the biblical Samson in the town's beautiful main square) in 1865.

STAROBRNO

BRNO

Records confirm that beer has been brewed around the site of Brno's major brewery – Starobrno – since about the time Robin Hood took refuge in Sherwood Forest in the middle of the thirteenth century. Between the fourteenth and nineteenth centuries, brewing on the Starobrno site was in the hands of monks in the monastery building still adjoining today's brewery, which dates only from 1872. It was built with share capital on the back of the beer boom which accompanied the industrial revolution. At the beginning of the twentieth century, Starobrno was producing almost 150,000 barrels a year. By the early 1990s it was one of ten largest breweries in the new Czech Republic. In a declining overall market, production rose in 1995 by 10 per cent to 585,000 hl (355,000 barrels).

Today's lack of rival breweries in the city stems from Starobrno's acquisitive activities in the 1920s and '30s – a factor which probably helped keep it alive during the nationalised years of the communist era. On a revised scale, the communists' command economy re-introduced the principles of the medieval "mile rights" royal ruling which curbed competition between brewers by preventing them selling their beer beyond a mile (in those days a Czech mile was almost five British miles) from the brewhouse. In communist Czechoslovakia, Starobrno – which means Old Brno – was Brno's monopoly supplier. Tough if you fancied something else. Perhaps as a backlash to that, the local brew is now not very commonplace in the city – freewheeling publicans and restaurateurs have gone out of their way to bring in outside choice. But that didn't dissuade Austrian brewing giant Brau Union AG from buying a 51 per cent controlling interest in Starobrno in September 1994. The rest of the business was still owned by the state in 1995, but it's the Austrians who have the money. Six beers are brewed at Starobrno: a pale 8 (3.2 abv) called Osma , three varieties of 10 degree – pale, dark, and Rezak, described as "half pale"- a pale 12 and a seasonal pale 14 called Drak (dragon).

Seventy per cent of the total is pale 10 (3.8 abv). The future of at least some of these beers must be uncertain following an announcement in autumn 1995 of plans to begin brewing Zipfer beer at Starobrno, one of Brau Union's big Austrian brands. It's a curious move. Czechs are still busy discovering all the native beers they were denied under the communists' local monopoly system and there has been some resistance to foreign brands. Starobrno's Austrian sales director Jurgen Frank says Zipfer will be no more expensive than Czech premium brands such as Pilsener Urquell – but why should it be? Austrian beer doesn't have more expensive ingredients, and in Brno its production costs can benefit from cheaper resources and local labour. Is it intended for export to Austria?

Starobrno beers are still fermented in big open squares, and the 12 degree beer is lagered for up to 12 weeks. But there are plans to introduce closed conical fermenters, and all beers have been pasteurised since the fad set in nationwide in the early 1990s. Moravian barley and Czech hops are used, plus up to five per cent brewing sugars.

The Austrians at Starobrno were also experimenting with the re-introduction of an unfiltered draught version of the brewery's pale 12 beer. Unfiltered beer used to be available in some Brno pubs which successfully demanded it even during the communist era. Brau Union have already supplied unfiltered versions of some of their Austrian beer to selected Viennese pubs. In German the unfiltered is known as Zwickelbier; in Czech kvasnicove pivo. In a back-handed acknowledgement that filtered, pasteurised beers were not necessarily what drinkers demand or want, Jurgen Frank was planning to call the brewery's unfiltered beer Sklepacki pivo – which means: the beer the brewery cellar workers drink.

STAROPRAMEN

SMICHOV, PRAGUE

The largest of Prague's five breweries is also the flagship of the privately owned Prazske Pivovary, or Prague Breweries. It is also known as the Smichov brewery, but more popularly Staropramen after the name of the beer brewed there. The other two breweries in the

Prague group are Branik, to the south, also beside the river, and Mestansky Pivovar, better known as Mestan, in Holesovice suburb a few kilometres north of Smichov. At the end of 1995, Prague Breweries held about ten per cent of the Czech domestic beer market.

Prague Breweries was created in 1992 in the first wave of privatisation after the demise of communism. Combined annual beer output of 2.3 million hl (1.4 million barrels) makes it the second largest brewing combine in the country, after the Pilsener Urquell Corporation. The company was fully Czech owned until late 1993 when one third of shares were bought by Britain's giant Bass company. That shareholding was increased to 39 per cent in late 1995. Bass is restricted to 46 per cent until the end of 1996, then everything is negotiable. The current deal brings in Bass investment capital and managerial expertise in production, marketing, sales and financial affairs. Bass managers shadow their Czech counterparts in Prague and some Bass executives sit on the Prague board.

Staropramen (1.3 million hl, 790,000 barrels) is a nineteenth-century brewery which grew up in Prague's workshop of Smichov, a grey tenemented district across the River Vltava from the more salubrious old city.

It was founded in 1869 as brewing industrialised to quench the collective thirst of a mushrooming urban society. At the end of 1995 it was still very much a traditional brewery with 140 open fermentation squares and classical small-scale horizontal lagering tanks.

Bass brewing adviser Steve

Denny, a microbiologist, is in favour of retaining the open fermentation method because he believes the primary fermentation process should have contact with the air in the fermentation room – and any house "character" which might be lurking there.

A new brewhouse is planned for early 1997 but it will be designed to allow the same cooking times and to retain oxidation, said Denny.

"When we arrived the Czechs were just going to buy a German system which excludes oxidation. We talked and we are going to have a modern brewery but with traditional Czech methods to produce the same beer only more efficiently. What we won't do is change the physical and chemical processes", he said.

Staropramen pale and dark are 100 per cent barley malt beers, 50 per cent of which comes from the brewery's own traditional floor maltings. The malthouse is separately located in Prague. The beers are fermented for seven days using two yeast strains: an original brewery culture and the ubiquitous W95 from the Weihenstephan laboratories near Munich. The brewing water comes from the adjacent Vltava River which is very soft – and clean. The brewery's own wells were closed because of iron contamination.

Bass claims credit for having persuaded the Czechs to halt plans to pasteurise and keg all draught beer for the domestic market. When Bass arrived they ordered more two-aperture aluminium casks which are needed for traditional air pressure dispense in pubs. That action followed a Bass survey of Prague drinkers which found considerable discontent about beer which had been gassed up with CO2 – part of the Czech brewing industry's embrace-all modernisation mania. But the Bass action only applies to big turnover pubs. Many new licensed premises since 1989 demand pasteurised and gassed beer because of low turnover and the need for longer shelf life.

The Staropramen 10 degree beer is lagered for three weeks and the 12 for a long 10 weeks.

Bass holds the right to market Staropramen abroad and in 1995 launched Staropramen pale 12, and later dark 12 in bottles, in Britain and other European countries. Batches destined for Britain are sent by refrigerated road tanker in an unfiltered form. The beer is then filtered, pasteurised and kegged in the UK. A pity they don't practise what they preach in Prague. Bass aims to sell 100,000 hl (60,000 barrels) a year in Britain alone, but says it will continue to be brewed only in Prague.

STRAKONICE

SOUTH BOHEMIA
Not one of the country's prettiest breweries, this hotch-potch of expanded buildings dates from the late nineteenth century although brewing in this town has a recorded history reaching back to the thirteenth century when the local manor was granted production rights by the Prague monarchy. The brewery has no maltings of its own and buys in malted Moravian barley plus Moravian hops.

During the communist era between 1948 and 1990, the Strakonice was part of the large ten-brewery South Bohemian conglomerate. But at the beginning of 1996, Strakonice and the breweries at Pelhrimov and Studena were still state owned because of disputes over pre-communist ownership and obscure brewing rights which go back to the Middle Ages.

Only three members of the communist-era group – Samson, Regent and Platan – broke away to form a privatised South Bohemian Breweries company.

Strakonice produces flavoursome 10, 11 and 12 beers, mainly under the brand name Nektar and sold mostly in the central-southern Bohemia region.

It's an example of a small, old brewery – capacity is about 200,000 hl (120,000 barrels) – with an uncertain future.

VELKE POPOVICE OR KOZEL

VELKE POPOVICE, 25 KM (16 MILES) SOUTHEAST OF PRAGUE

At first scrutiny, Popovice seems to be the people's brewery of the new capitalist Bohemia. When it was privatised, it acquired more than 25,000 small shareholders who chipped in 300 million crowns (about £7.5 million). The 1993 share issue was over-subscribed – a reflection of the nationwide popularity of the brewery's beers. The bad news for beer drinkers is that Popovice's biggest shareholder with 13 per cent (1995) is Radegast, the mushrooming brewing giant to the east in Moravia. Since that heady rush of the new Czech share-owning society – not unlike the Thatcher privatisations of the British public utilities – Popovice has become a partner in a Whitbread-like protective umbrella, something described as the Radegast Group. The brewery at Most in northern Bohemia was also part of this cooperative partnership. In late 1995, Most was gobbled up completely by Radegast when a general shareholders' meeting agreed to change the brewery's name to Radegast Sedlec. Most was operating below capacity even though it already produced Radegast dark 10. The Radegast aim is to target more of the Prague market via Most.

The Popovice brewery was conceived in 1871 by the German-speaking Prague industrialist Franz Ringhoffer who bought an impoverished squire's country estate, then called Gross Popowitz, later Czechified to Velke Popovice. Brewing on the estate had been going on since at least the seventeenth century. Ringhoffer had a rather idealistic self sufficiency plan: grow the hops and barley, brew the beer, feed the spent waste to cattle. He died before the plan was realised, but his three sons put it into practice. The brewery became highly successful and between the world wars was producing 350,000 (212,000 barrels) a year.

Up until 1995, Popovice remained a traditional producer – open fermentation, horizontal lagering in small scale tanks, unpasteurised beer on demand – but at the end of 1995 general manager Jiri Kozak heralded changes when he spoke in the Czech beer newspaper Pivni Kuryr about "moving from classical production to large scale capacity." He talked about his learning experiences at the Japanese brewing giant Kirin where he had discovered the "delicate finesse of conical fermenters…"

In 1994, Popovice's total annual production reached 930,000 hl – about five per cent of the total Czech beer market – but the brewery made no profit. The goal for 1995 was 1.2 million hl (730,000 barrels). Popovice is one of the few Czech breweries to date which has also invested in pub ownership. Its small estate includes several in Prague and Plzen and the goal is about 120 tied pubs across western Bohemia.

The brewery concentrates on three beers: pale 10 and 12 and dark 10, which was re-introduced only in 1991 and, contrary to general industry views of Czech drinkers' conservatism, is increasingly popular. The bulk of production reflects the national trend to weaker, cheaper beer – pale 10.

Kozel* beers will prosper, in the short-medium term because they are flavoursome, popular brands, but the relationship with the predatory Radegast must be cause for concern for beer lovers.

*It means billy goat – the brewery's emblem.

ZATEC

ZATEC TOWN, NORTHERN BOHEMIA

This small, cash-starved but proud brewery sits on the site of a castle at the top of Zatec's main square, where it has been brewing since 1801, although the history of brewing in this capital of the hop-growing region is known to reach back to at least 1200. Inevitably, the brewery claims the slogan: "Beer From The Town of The Hops".

The brewery was sold to a single buyer during 1995 for 50 million crowns – £1,250,000. In mid 1995 the brewery looked like a museum, but the new owner was said to have bold plans for its rejuvenation, including a pub-hotel with beer garden within the brewery grounds, and a new dark beer. In 1995, Zatec produced only three beers, all pale and hoppy – 10, 11 and 12.

Zatec is one of the smallest of the country's old established breweries with an annual capacity of 100,000 hl (60,000 barrels). It is probably operating well under capacity, but it is a survivor. Before the demise of the communist state in 1989, the brewery had been earmarked for closure. It had suffered from years of under-investment with profits being redistributed elsewhere.

Brewing methods are very traditional: open fermentation, horizontal lagering tanks in cellars cut into the hill on which the old town stands above the hop-growing plain. Up to mid 1995, all draught beer was sent out unpasteurised in air-vented aluminium casks for traditional air dispense, but there were plans to introduce a new kegging line. Brewer Miroslav Hervert said new retailers in lower-turnover outlets demanded the longer shelf life and stability provided by pasteurisation and CO_2 dispense.

Zatec has its own maltings and produces more than it needs; some is bought by the Krusovice brewery. The two-row barley is from northern Bohemia. Zatec hops are used in both pellet and extract form because, says the brewer, the brewery doesn't have the equipment to handle whole hops. Town water is used.

The 10 degree beer (called Zatecka Desitka) – which accounts for 77 per cent of production – is lagered for three and a half weeks; the 12 for six and a half. Despite 10's domination, brewer Hervert says the drinkers' favourite is the 11 (called Lucan – no connection with the missing English earl, it's an ancient local tribal name). The name for the 12 – Chmelar – means hop picker.

Entrance to Budvar brewery, under the old regime

MICROS

One of the pluses of the free market in Czech brewing has been the emergence of brew pubs, or micro-breweries. There is nothing original in this; it is yet another embrace by the Czechs of western trends. But to a small extent it provides a counter-balance to the concentration and inevitable reduction of choice in the old-established Czech brewing industry.

The sad truth about brew pubs and micro-breweries, however, is that they tend to develop only when a country's mainstream brewing industry has imploded, or is beginning to implode. Since 1992, miniature breweries have appeared across the country, in both big city and small country town. It is difficult to ascertain exactly how many there are because some are not registered with any organisation and public relations is not yet very sophisticated even among some entrepreneurial Czechs. Industry sources estimate there are probably between fifteen and eighteen micros in operation. Some have opened only to close a few months later. One such was the Bavorsky brewery in Brno. Its owners got their sums wrong, and the location in a poor outer suburb was probably not the smartest business move. Curiously, it had been brewing a Bavarian beer under licence. The good news is that the brewing equipment from the failed Bavorsky is now operating again 160 km (100 miles) distant at Tabor in central Bohemia.

Some Czech micros have risen from the ruins of former age-old breweries, as at Zvikov Pohradi and Kacov in central Bohemia. One or two, having set up in low-cost, semi-rural surroundings, are coping with seasonal trading slumps by running their brewery in conjunction with some other business activity such as a bakery, or hotel. At Zvikovske Podhradi, they make bread, sausages and offer lodgings. The micro-brewery at Kacov, south-east of Prague, has been built in an old brewery which closed in 1957. It is produces four pale and dark beers and serves them in the old brewery's converted maltings hall.

The Novomestsky Pivovar in Prague and the Pegas Pivovar in Brno have thrived from day one, although it would difficult not to succeed given their central locations in the two biggest cities. But neither of these relies solely on beer sales to survive; both serve a lot of meals and Pegas also has bed and breakfast accommodation.

Virtually all the new Czech brew pubs produce fairly standard 10 or 12 pale or dark bottom-fermenting beers, but mostly also unfiltered. A constant refrain in the brewing industry is that Czech beer drinkers are conservative and reluctant to try new styles. As the mainstream Czech brewing industry moves inexorably towards mass-produced pale, pasteurised lager, it will be for the micros to prove this claim to be false. The Pegas micro (it serves pubs other than its own) in Brno showed the way by producing one beer flavoured with ginger, plus a wheat beer. And at the beginning of 1996, the Pivovar Excellent at Rymarov, in northern Moravia began brewing a rich, dark unfiltered 14 degree beer.

The problem with some of the Czech micro-breweries is that lack of lagering space or pressure of economics, or both, results in beer being served "green" or immature.

The equipment for many of these new brewing operations comes from a Czech firm called ZVU, in Hradec Kralove, which is now also exporting its micro-brewery packages, not least to Germany and Japan. ZVU has supplied equipment to the country's standard-sized breweries for a number of years, but the move into micros was classic swords-to-ploughshares – it had to find an alternative to armaments manufacture in the post-Cold War era.

ZVU produces two micro sizes: one offering an annual capacity between 1,000 and 5,000 hl (600-3,000 barrels) a year; the other up 10,000 hl. If anyone out there is interested in chancing their luck in Czech brewing, prices begin at around £200,000. The Czech beer newspaper Pivni Kuryr quoted unnamed industry "experts" in 1995 estimating that there is probably room in the Czech market place for up to fifty micro-breweries. That seems to be an over-optimistic figure in the present economic climate of the country.

These are the towns with brew pubs or micros reported to have been operating at the end of 1995, although a question mark hangs over several, including Chyne. An asterisk indicates that the beer is obtainable in a Prague pub:

Belec nad Orlici, 8 km (5 miles) east of Hradec Kralove, north-east Bohemia

Boskovice, northern Moravia

Brno

Chyne, north-west of Prague just outside the city limits. Possibly closed.

Hodonin, 50 km (31 miles) south-east of Brno

Hlucin, near Ostrava in north-east Moravia

Hradec Kralove (the U Zezulaku in Malsovice district), north-east Bohemia

Kacov * (in U Bergneru – see Prague Pubs) , south-east of Prague along Brno motorway

Novy Jicin, between Olomouc and Ostrava in Moravia

Prague Novomestsky pivovar – see Prague Pubs

Pruhonice * (in U Bezousku – see Prague Pubs)

Rymarov, near Sumperk north of Olomouc, Moravia

Roznov pod Radhostem, east Moravia, near Valasske

Mezirici.

Svinistany (the U Lipy) between Jaromer and Nachod in north-east Bohemia

Tabor, southern Bohemia

Vitkov, 40 km (25 miles) west of Ostrava in Moravia

Vrchlabi, north-east Bohemia, near Trutnov

Zvikovske Podhradi * (in Cerny Pivovar – see Prague Pubs), near Pisek, southern Bohemia

"Wouldn't it be easier if your husband came to the pub himself?"

TASTING NOTES

The chief names (in capitals) listed below are the most common identifications in general marketing use for the breweries and their beers. Often this is the new name of the brewery, as with Bernard. Sometimes it is the beer brand itself, as with Staropramen or Budweiser Budvar. On other occasions it is simply the name of the brewery town, for example Domazlice or Louny. The number after the beer name (e.g. Ferdinand pale 10) is the Czech degrees Balling system of indicating strength. The figure in brackets is the alcohol by volume (ABV) given by the breweries.

BENESOV

Bohemia, just south of Prague Part of the five-brewery private group Pivovary Bohemia Praha (Bohemia Breweries Prague – not to be confused with Prague Breweries), whose flagship brand is a new beer called Old Bohemia. The others in the Benesov group are at Rakovnik, Podkovan, Nymburk and Kutna Hora.
FERDINAND PALE 10 (3.7) Deep golden. Faint malt aroma. A sharp, slightly sweet-malt taste. ★
FERDINAND DARK 11 (4.1) Dark brown. Little aroma, but a firm malty flavour. Full bodied with a bitter-sweet finish. ★★

BERNARD

Humpolec, south-east of Prague
PALE 12 (5.1) Deep golden. Bitter-sweet taste and a long dry finish. ★★
DARK 11 (4.9) Light brown. Full-bodied malty dry flavour and a long aftertaste. ★★★

BRANIK

Prague, part of Prague Breweries group
PALE 12 (4.6) Very pale. Initial hop bitterness becomes sweeter. Bitter-sweet finish. ★★

STAR RATING ★★★★★
OUTSTANDING ★★★
EXCELLENT ★★
GOOD ★
AVERAGE ★

DARK 10 (3.6) Chestnut brown. Light malt aroma. Light bodied with a malty-sweet finish. ★

BUDWEISER BUDVAR

Ceske Budejovice, south Bohemia
BUDVAR 12 (5.0) Copper coloured. A rich malty aroma over a full-bodied beer with a soft bitter-sweet finish. ★★★★ The brewery also produces a 10 degree (4.1) version which is being increasingly distributed in the domestic market and an 8 degree Budvar "light" (3.0) primarily for Sweden.

CERNA HORA

Cerna Hora, near Brno in Moravia
HARDY (3.2) Very pale. Thin in body and taste, but with a clean refreshing finish. A summer drink. ★
TAS (2.8) Pale golden. Very yeasty nose. Malty taste with a slightly bitter-dry finish. ★★
CERNOHORSKY LEZAK (3.5) Deeper golden than Tas. Little

aroma. Full-bodied, bitter-sweet taste. ★★

GRANAT (3.5) Dark brown. No aroma. Very malty taste and sweetish finish with a long malty aftertaste. ★★

CHODOVAR

Chodova Plana, north-west Bohemia near Marianske Lazne

DARK 10 (3.8) Tawny colour. Little aroma but a lightly flavoured, nutty-dry beer with a crisp finish. ★★

DOMAZLICE

South-west Bohemia, close to border with Bavaria
Part of Pilsner Urquell Corporation

PRIOR WHEAT (KVASNICOVE, 5.0) Deep amber. Unfiltered. Very yeasty aroma. Very dry with a bitter, spicy flavour. ★★★

PURKMISTR 12 (4.8) Almost black. Malty aroma. Initial sweetness develops into a rich coffee-bitter dryness. A coarse textured beer in the mouth. ★★★

A Purkmistr 10 is also produced.

EGGENBERG

Ceske Krumlov, south Bohemia
All four beers have the same trade name: Eggenberg. In bottles, label colours define the type. Diet beer is not listed here. Available mostly in south Bohemia, plus one or two outlets in Prague.

PALE 10 (4) Straw coloured. Little aroma but a gentle hoppy taste and dryish finish. ★★

DARK 10 (4) Tawny-brown. Little aroma. Malty-dry flavour and a clean finish. Full-bodied feel for a 10 degree beer. ★★

PALE 12 (5) Straw coloured. Hoppy aroma. Full-bodied, hoppy flavour with a firm, dry finish. ★★★

GAMBRINUS

Pilsen
Part of Pilsner Urquell Corporation

PALE 10 (4.1) Very pale. Slightly malty aroma. Clean, dryish flavour with slight bitterness in the aftertaste. ★★

PALE 12 (5.1) Very pale. Slightly fruity, firm bodied and hoppy with a clean, dryish finish. ★★

PRIMUS 10 (3.8) Light golden. Hoppy aroma, thin bodied, bitter-sweet palate and finish. ★

HEROLD

Breznice, south of Prague

PALE 10 (3.8) Straw coloured. Hoppy aroma, crisp, clean taste with a dry bitterish bite. ★★

PALE 12 (4.8) Bronze. Firm hop aroma. Fuller bodied than pale 10 but same clean dry finish. ★★★

HEROLD WHEAT (5.2) The colour of set honey. Lemony aroma. A dry sourness mostly devoid of the sweet-sour complexity of Bavarian wheat beers. Finally very dry. ★★★

DARK 13 (5.2) Coal black. Malty aroma with a hint of hops. Initial coffeeish flavour becomes malty-dry with a long, dry aftertaste. A very full-bodied flavoursome beer. ★★★★

HOSTAN

Znojmo, on Moravian border with Austria

PALE 12 (4.8) Pale golden. Full-bodied lager beer with a dry, bitterish flavour and aftertaste. ★★

GRANAT 10 (4.0) Tawny brown. Malty aroma. Rich, coffeeish, full-bodied taste finishing slightly

bitter ★★★
Pale 10 and 11 versions are also
produced for the local market.

JAROSOV

Uherske Hradiste, south Moravia
PREMIUM (5.3) Bronze coloured
winter season only. Fruity aroma.
Dry tasting with a bitter edge.
★★
PALE 12 (4.8) Lemon coloured.
Malty aroma and malty-dry
flavour and long aftertaste.
★★★
DARK 11 (3.9) Medum brown.
Hoppy aroma. Caramel flavour
which dries to a clean crisp
finish. ★★

JIHLAVA

Moravia, north-west of Brno.
Bought by Austrian brewers
Zwettl in 1995
JEZEK PALE 11 (3.8) Rich bronze
colour. Hint of lemon in the
aroma. Fruity-dry with a crisp
finish. ★★★
DARK 10 (3.4) Dark brown.
Hoppy aroma, brief chocolaty
flavour which fades. ★★

KARLOVY VARY

Part of Pilsner Urquell group
KAREL IV PALE 11 (4.0) Pale
golden. Fruity nose and a fruity-
dry taste and finish. ★★

KOZEL (VELKE POPOVICE)

Velke Popovice, south-east of
Prague
KOZEL PALE 12 (5) Lemony
colour. Hoppy and dry tasting
with a hint of fruitiness at the
end. ★★★
KOZEL DARK 10 (4.3) Dark
brown. Malty aroma. Full-tasting
and fruity-dry beer. ★★★

KRUSOVICE

Rakovnik, west of Prague
The German brewing giant
Binding owns a 51 per cent
shareholding
PALE 12 (5.1) Very pale. Short,
bitter-sweet taste. ★
DARK 10 (3.7) Very dark brown.
Initial malt-sweetness, drying out
in a thin finish. ★

LITOVEL

Litovel, southern Moravia
Part of Moravian-Silesian
Breweries group
PALE 12 (5.1) Corn coloured.
Fruity aroma. Soft, light bodied
pale lager, with a dryish finish.
★★

LOBKOWICZY

Vysoky Chlumec, central
Bohemia
Close trading links with Austrian
giant Brau AG
PALE 12 (5.0) Pale golden. Faint
hop aroma. Clean tasting
without much depth of flavour.
Dry finish. ★
DARK 12 (4.6) Ruby-brown.
Roasted malt aroma leading into
a caramel-malty flavour and a
bitter edged finish. ★★

LOUNY

Louny, northern Bohemia in hop
growing district
PALE 10 (3.4) Very pale golden.
Hint of malt in the nose but a
hoppy flavoured and dry beer.
★★
DARK 12 (4.3) Dark brown.
Malty aroma. Firm bodied and
smooth with a malty finish. ★★

MESTAN

Holesovice, Prague
Part of Prague Breweries group

PRAGOVAR PALE 12 (4.9) Deep golden. Yeasty aroma. Light malty flavour and hoppy background taste before a bitter-sweet finish. ★★

MESTAN DARK 11 (4.1) Dark brown. Roasted malt aroma. A firm-bodied, malty beer. Bitter-sweet finish. ★★

NACHOD

Nachod, north-east Bohemia, on Polish border
A range of beers all bearing the brand name Primator. The two listed here are also sold in the London area.

PRIMATOR PREMIUM (PALE 12, 5.1) Deep golden. Firm lemony aroma and taste. A crisp beer with an edge of bitterness and a long dry finish and aftertaste. ★★★

PRIMATOR DARK 12 (5.1) Medium brown. Chocolate-malt aroma and taste with a long dry finish and aftertaste. ★★★

NOVOMESTSKY

Prague brew pub
PALE 11 (4) Russet colour, unfiltered. Slightly fruity aroma, but cloyingly sweet taste.★

OLOMOUC

Olomouc, central Moravia
Part of Moravian-Silesian Breweries
Beers sold mainly in the Moravian region.

HOLAN 10 (3.5) Amber colour. Unfiltered version tasted: yeasty aroma, very hoppy taste ending fruity-dry. Lip-smacking aftertaste. ★★★

VACLAV 12 (5.6) Amber. Slight hoppy aroma, hint of malt in the mouth. Bitter-sweet finish. ★★

GRANAT 12 (5.6) Deep Burgundy colour. Coffee-like aroma. Rich malty flavour. Long, dry aftertaste. ★★★★

OSTRAVAR

Ostrava, north-east Moravia
Bought by Bass in 1995
ONDRAS PALE 12 (5.2) Deep golden. Hoppy aroma. Crisp, hoppy taste with bitter-sweet finish. ★★

VRANIK PORTER 10 (3.8) Chestnut brown. Burnt malt aroma and taste and long, dry finish. ★★★

A pale 10 called Konik was not tasted.

PEGAS

Brew pub, Brno, southern Moravia
GINGER BEER (4) Reddish colour. Unfiltered. Ginger-peppery aroma. Soft textured beer, mild flavoured with a very dry finish. ★★★

PALE (4) Unfiltered, reddish colour. Slight yeasty aroma. Soft but full bodied with a bitter-sweet finish. ★★

DARK (4) Very dark brown. Caramel aroma. A chewy, coarse beer, initially malty, finishing fruity-dry.★★★

PARDUBICE

Pardubice, east of Prague
PORTER 19 (7) Reputedly the strongest regularly brewed beer in the country.
Very dark ruby. Liquorice aroma. Initial heavy malty-sweetness dries out to leave a fruity edge and aftertaste. ★★

PILSNER URQUELL

Pilsen
PILSNER URQUELL 12 (4.4) Golden. Some hop and malt aroma. Firm hoppy taste and a

bitter-dry finish which lingers long in the aftertaste. Sharper and perhaps thinner in 1995 than before brewing methods changed. ★★★

PLATAN

Protivin
Part of the South Bohemian Breweries group (Samson & Regent)
The brewery produces three pale beers of 10, 11 and 12 strength, plus a dark 10. All four are simply called Platan.
PLATAN PALE 10 (3.9) Copper coloured and darked of the three pales. Light hoppy aroma and taste. ★
PLATAN PALE 12 (5.0) Very light golden. Firm hoppy aroma. Firmer bodied than 10 and 11. Good dry, hoppy finish. ★★
PLATAN DARK 10 (3.6) Dark chestnut colour. Slightly burnt malt aroma. Surprisingly full bodied malty-dry taste and a bitterish finish. ★★

PREROV

south Moravia
Part of Moravian-Silesian group
ZUBR PALE 10 (3.8) Deep golden. Hoppy aroma. Light bodied, slightly malty taste and bitter-sweet finish. ★

PROSTEJOV

Prostejov, southern Moravia, east of Brno
Most of the brewery's beers are marketed under the name Jecminek, a legendary Moravian king. The ABV strengths shown here were given by the brewery, but seem doubtful.
JECMINEK PALE 12 (3.1) Lemony colour. Hoppy aroma. Light bodied with a slightly fruity flavour, finishing crisp and dry with an edge of bitterness. ★★
JECMINEK PALE 14 (3.6) Deep copper. Firm hoppy aroma, crisp, dry bitterish taste. ★★

RADEGAST

Nosovice district of Frydek-Mistek, north Moravia
RADEGAST PALE 12 (5.1) Golden. Faint fruity aroma, dryish taste and finish. Easy drinking beer. ★★
RADEGAST DARK 10 (3.6) Dark brown. Malty with a slightly burnt caramel edge. Sweetish finish. ★★

REGENT

Trebon
Part of South Bohemian Breweries group
Regent's five pale and one dark are marketed under the same name of Bohemia Regent. In bottles, label colour defines the type. The dark is marketed in Britain as Black Regent. Pale 10 and 12 are the most common domestically; some of the other pale varieties are for export only.
REGENT DARK 12 (4.2) Coal black. Liquorice aroma, slightly burnt malt flavour. Full bodied with a dryish finish. ★★★★
BOHEMIA REGENT 12 (4.8) Copper coloured. Yeasty aroma and taste with a hint of fruitiness. Crisp, dryish finish. ★★★
BOHEMIA REGENT 10 (3.5) Slightly darker than 12, and noticeably thinner but with a refreshing dry taste. ★★

SAMSON

Ceske Budejovice
Part of South Bohemian Breweries
DARK 10 (3.6) Tawny-brown. Little aroma, but a refreshing

malty-dry flavour. Slight coffee-like finish. In local pubs often mixed half and half with pale 10. ★★

PALE 10 (4.0) Deep golden. Hoppy aroma. Thin body but a crisp, clean tasting beer with a dry finish. ★★

Pale 11. Sometimes called Samson Gold (4.6)
Copper coloured. Hoppy aroma, dry flavour and bitterish aftertaste. ★★

Pale 12. Sometimes marketed abroad as Crystal. (5.2)
The deep copper colour is unusually dark for a Czech "pale". Hoppy aroma, full bodied and slightly fruity with a crisp, dry, clean finish. ★★

STAROBRNO

Brno
Owned by Austrian giant Brau AG
Major market is in Moravia but under the new Austrian management it will become more nationally available. In Prague at the Ibero (see Prague – Pubs). The unfiltered Premium is occasionally available in Brno.

PREMIUM (5.1) Very pale golden 12. Malty aroma and full-bodied malty taste with a bitter-sweet finish. ★★★

PALE 10 (3.8) Some hop aroma and flavour with dryish finish ★★

Premium unfiltered
More full-bodied than the filtered version, with a fruity, drier flavour and slighty bitter aftertaste. ★★★

KARAMELOVE 10 (3.8) Dark brown. Hoppy aroma, clean tasting with a malty-dry finish. ★★

DRAK (DRAGON, 5.9) Dark Christmas season brew, matured for four months. Chocolatey-rich and malty. ★★★

STAROPRAMEN

Smichov, Prague
Part of Prague Breweries group, part-owned by Bass

STAROPRAMEN PALE 12 (5) Very pale golden. Distinctive hop flower aroma. Firm hoppy and malty flavours. Crisp dry finish with a light bitterness in the aftertaste. ★★★

STAROPRAMEN DARK 12 (4.6) Dark brown/ruby. Liquorice aroma. Rich burnt malt taste edged with bitterness and a long malty-dry finish and aftertaste. ★★

STRAKONICE

Southern Bohemia
The name Nektar applies to three beers: pale 10 and 11 and dark 10. The dark was not tasted. Sold mostly in central-southern Bohemia.

NEKTAR PALE 10 (3.8) Pale straw colour. Fruity aroma and quite full-bodied for a 10. Very dry finish ★★

DUDAK PALE 12 (4.8) Pale golden. Vanilla-like aroma. Rich and firm bodied with a dry, slightly bitter aftertaste. ★★★

U FLEKU

Prague brew pub
FLEKOVSKY DARK 13 (5.5) Almost black. Malt and yeast in the aroma. A thick, rich brew. Initially malty-sweet but drying out in a lip-smacking spicy finish. ★★★

VYSKOV

Vyskov, southern Moravia, east of Brno
HAVRAN DARK 11 (3.6) Dark brown. Liquorice aroma and flavour with a sweet-malt finish. ★★

DZBAN PALE 11 (3.9) Straw coloured. Hoppy aroma with a malty taste and a slightly bitter edge. ★★

BREZNAK PALE 12 (4.8) Pale amber. Slightly yeasty aroma. A hoppy tasting beer with a dry finish. ★★

ZATEC

Zatec, northern Bohemia
DESITKA (3.1) Very pale. Light on the mouth with a crisp dry aftertaste. ★
LUCAN (3.6) Pale golden. Surprisingly full-bodied and fruity. Soft finish and gently hoppy aftertaste. ★★★
CHMELAR (4.2) Deep golden. More bitterness than Lucan and a drier, harder finish. ★★

ZLATOVAR (OPAVA)

Opava, southern Moravian
Part of Moravian-Silesian Breweries group
ZLATOVAR PALE 12 (5.1) Bronze coloured. Slightly malty aroma. Malty-dry taste with a bitter edge. Dry finish. ★★★
A 10 degree version is also produced.

Cesky Krumlov from the castle walls

GENERAL INFORMATION

GENERAL INFO

Watch out for cheap specials with British Airways and Lufthansa to Munich and Vienna, which have good train and bus connections with the Czech Republic.
An almost daily bus service operates between London and Prague. Contact Kingscourt Express (KCE), 15 Balham High Road, London SW12 9AJ, tel 0181 673-7500, fax 673-3060.

Prospective purchasers of the Eurail Pass should check whether it now covers the Czech Republic.

General travel and accommodation information is available from the London offices of Cedok Travel Ltd, the former Czech state version of Thomas Cook's, now privatised: 53 Haymarket, London SW1Y 4RP, tel 0171 839-4414, fax 839-0204.

IN AN EMERGENCY

Throughout the country, dial 158 for Police and 155 for quick medical help such as an ambulance.

The word or sign for a chemist's shop is Lekarna. Most are open until 1800 Mon-Fri, but only until 1200 on Saturdays. In Prague, two which remain open 24 hours are at Na prikope 7, Prague 1 (bottom end of Wenceslas Square), and Lekarna U andela, Stefanikova 6, Prague 5. It's between the Lesser Town and Smichov. Take Metro B (yellow line) to Andel station.

For urgent medical help outside Prague, ask for the nearest hospital – nemocnice (nem-ots-nyi-tse), or dial 155 for an ambulance. A key help word is: pain – bolest (boll-est).

In Prague, English-speaking assistance is available 24 hours at: Health Care Unlimited in the poliklinika, Revolucni 19 , Prague 1 (Metro B to namesti Republiky). There may be a consultation charge.

If you are hopelessly lost on the map or have suffered a theft, key words for help are: lost – ztraceny (stratt-senn-ee), police policie (pol-it-see-e), stolen – ukradny (oo-krad-nee).

Embassies: British – Thunovska 14, Prague 1. Consulate section, for passport losses etc: tel 536-737. United States – Trziste 15, Prague 1, tel 536-641. Both embassies can be reached via the Metro to Malostranska station.

CURRENCY

The Czech unit of currency is the koruna (crown). The abbreviation is: kc. The koruna is divided into 100 heller. There are about 40 to the British pound, 18-20 to the German mark, and 25-28 to the U.S. dollar. For cash exchange, marks are often preferred and you may get a better rate than for pounds. In some private guest houses, especially in rural Bohemia, you may be asked to pay in marks. Beware of worthless old Czechoslovak koruna which may be still in circulation.

CAR HIRE

Unless travelling in your own car, it is best to hire locally if you want to explore Bohemia. A car in Prague is not very practical, so if you do take your own park it up safely while staying in the city (see Car Security in Prague chapter). Be careful if you hire a car in a neighbouring western country such as Germany or Austria and plan to drive in the Czech Republic – some hire firms will no longer provide insurance cover for the Czech Republic because of the risk of theft. In Prague, international firms such as Avis and Hertz charge western rates; local firms are cheaper. Several worth trying are: Pragocar, tel 692-2875; Unix, tel 233-693; Rent A Car, tel 2422-9848.

TELEPHONING

Czech numbers given in this guide are mostly the local number only (in the case of Prague), or the area code and local number, on the assumption that readers will make calls to book accommodation or a tour within the country as you travel. To phone or fax from abroad, the Czech national code is 0042. The Prague code is 2. And as elsewhere, if dialling from abroad you drop the initial zero in area codes.

Many public call boxes in Prague can be used only with a phone card. Calls are very cheap so a 50 crown card is sufficient for local calls; by them at Post Offices or newspaper kiosks. For long distance and international calls either buy a more expensive card (up to 300 crowns) or go to a Post Office where you can book a call and pay cash at the end. Coin-operated boxes use a variety of coins. Put the money in, dial the number.

OTHER READING

The most informative general guide to Prague is Time Out Prague. The best detailed guide to the rest of the country, especially for castle spotters, is the AA/Baedeker's Czech/Slovak Republic's Guide. In the capital, the English language broadsheet Prague Post has sections for visitors and offers an excellent weekly snapshot of the country. To order copies (£1.50 each) ahead of a visit, tel 0042-2-248 75016, fax 248-75050.

EATING

Everyday Czech cuisine is similar to neighbouring Germany and Austria – pork in various forms, potatoes, dumplings, and side salad. The quality and servings, especially in pubs, have increased enormously since Communist times. And for westerners pub dining remains very cheap – for a main course roast meal £2 or less in an average Prague pub; less than £1 in rural Bohemia. The staples are relieved by some tasty sausages and delicious spicy potato cakes called bramboraky. Fish is also increasingly available. The Bohemian speciality is carp (kapr), which can come plain grilled or baked in batter and in a variety of sauces. Try it with some Regent black beer from Trebon. In Moravia, traditional dishes can be quite piquant with the liberal use of paprika. See Vocabulary chapter for some meal suggestions.

Customs

SHOP HOURS: Monday-Friday 0830-1830; in small towns they may close at lunchtime; Saturday 0830-1300 only.

IN THE PUB: apart from obvious stand-up bars and railway or bus station cafeterias, most pubs expect you to sit before being served. This means joining strangers at a table if there are no completely empty tables – even if they are eating. As in most other mainland European countries, you pay for all you have had – drinks and food – only when you leave. Most waiters will mark your beer mat with a pen slash or cross each time you order a beer. Some pubs have a standing area beside the beer fonts and the beer may be cheaper there, but sometimes these areas are reserved for the locals. It depends on the pub staff. If you sit down, you have to be patient about being served. Sometimes this may take a few minutes; in some pubs a beer will automatically be brought to you without ordering.

TIPPING: It is customary to round up your bill by a crown or two – or more if you have enjoyed good friendly service.

East-West: Despite the Czech Republic's race to embrace "western values", putting it well ahead of other former Iron Curtain countries in market economy terms, some general travel guides to the country have painted a picture of a Third World culture with a moral code distorted by forty years of Communism. This is arrogant western nonsense. The Czechs are, by and large, a gentle, civilised people. Excluding Prague taxi drivers, Czechs are no less, and no more, honest than the rest of us.

Traditional oak fermenting casks at Pilsner Urquell – now replaced by conical steel vessels

VOCABULARY GUIDE

Czech seems to be an impenetrable row of consonants. The language uses the Roman alphabet but has many special diphthongs and uses diacritics to modify the pronunciation of some consonants. Added to these, Czech has seven case endings. The letters l and r are used as vowels and many vocal stresses are made with both letters. The vowels a, e, i, o, u, are similar to northern English pronunciation, as in bed, bit, cat, cot, cut. An acute accent (´) or a small circle - the krouzek - (°) over a vowel lengthens them. y is a vowel similar to i. The hacek, pronounced "hat-check" - (˅) over an e indicates a sound like an English y.

Consonants are similar to English, except:
c = ts in cats
c = ch in church
d = j in jug
ch = Scottish loch
j = y in yet
n = ny in canyon
r = sound between r in red and s in leisure
s = sh in ship
t = ch in cheese
z = s in leisure

Word stress is always on the first syllable, except when a preposition precedes the word; then the preposition takes the stress.

Perhaps most confusing of all for a student of Czech is the spoken word for yes: it sounds like aah-no. To add to the mystery, if you have learnt some standard Czech, there are strong dialects in both Bohemia and Moravia, as well as 200,000 gypsies roving the country speaking pure Romany. But at least it's quite easy to sound friendly. The word for a general greeting is a simple, nautical ahoy!

Together with Slovak and Polish, Czech forms part of the so-called western branch of the Slavonic languages.

Until the Velvet Revolution of late 1989, the first foreign language for Czechs was Russian. Since then, English and German have replaced Russian on the school curriculum. In Prague, an increasing number of people in the tourist industry speak some English, but they are by no means fluent; often their vocabulary will be closely linked to the service they are involved in - serving food, providing beds, or directing you to the castle. So don't be surprised if an uncomprehending blank stare results from a piece of flattery like: "You have such beautiful eyes, I want to pack you in my suitcase and smuggle you back home."

Outside Prague, very little English is spoken but many people - especially the older generation - understand and can speak limited German. The reason for this is that until 1945-6 there were an estimated 3.5 million German-speaking people living in the country.

In fact, until independence from the Austrian Hapsburg empire in 1918 the official language was German.

An estimated 50,000 German speakers still live in the Karlovy Vary-Cheb and Liberec-Trutnov districts, but the rest of those 3.5 million were driven out by the Czechs in the chaos at the end of the Second World War.

In the following simple vocabulary guide, Czech words are also shown phonetically – within parentheses – to aid pronunciation.

BEER MATTERS

beer – pivo (piv-o)
    desitka (de-seet-ka), *a beer of 10 degree strength*
    jednactka (yed-naatst-ka), *11 degree beer*
    dvanactka (dva-naatst-ka), *12 degree beer*
    lezak (le-zhaak), *11 degree or over*
bottled beer – lahvove pivo (la-hvo-vey piv-o)
brewery – pivovar
cellar – sklep
closed – zavreno (zav-zhre-no)
daily – kazdy den (kazh-dee den)
dark beer- tmave pivo (dmaa-vey piv-o) or cerne pivo
    (cherr-ney piv-o)
draught – tocine pivo (totch-e-ney piv-o) or cepovane pivo
    (che-po-va-ney piv-o)
food – jidlo (yeed-lo)
garden – zahrada (za-hra-da) or zahradka (za-hrad-ka)
mixed beer (half pale, half dark) – rezani (zhre-za-nyee)
opening times – oteviraci doba (ot-e-vee-ra-tsee dob-a)
pale- svetle pivo (zvyet-ley piv-o)
pub – hospoda (hosp-o-da) or hostinec (hos-ti-nets) or pivnice
    (piv-nyit-se)
unfiltered beer – kvasnicove pivo (gvass-nyits-oh-vey piv-o)
wheat beer – psenicove pivo (pshe-nits-oh-vey piv-o)

MEAL TIME

baked – pecene (petch-e-ney)
beef – hovezi (hov-ye-zee)
boiled – vareni (vazr-ye-nyee)
breakfast – snidane (snyee-da-nye)
cabbage – zeli (ze-lee)
carp – kapr (kap-rr)
cheese – syr (seerr)
chicken – kure (koozr-ye)
coffee – kava (ka-va)
cold dishes – studene jidlo (stoo-de-ney yee-dlo)
dumplings – knedliky (gned-lee-ky)
eggs – vejce (ve-iy-tse)

fish – ryby (ri-bi)
fried – smazene (sma-zhe-ney)
game – zverina (zvyezr-yi-na)
hot dishes – tiple jidlo (tep-ley yee-dlo)
quick dishes – minutka
menu – jidelni listek (yee-dell-nyee lee-stek)
milk – mleko (mley-ko)
pork – veprove (vep-rsho-vey)
potatoes – brambory
sausage – klobasy
tea – caj (chai)
vegetables – zelenina (ze-le-nyr-na)

PUB DISHES

bramboraky – *spicy potato cakes* (bram-bo-rraa-ky)
gulas – *goulash* (goo-laash)
langos – *savoury pancake fritter* (lang-osh)
ovocne knedliky – *fruit dumpling* (ov-ots-ney gned-lee-ky)
sekana – *meat loaf* (sekk-a-naa)
svickova – *beef in cream sauce* (zveech-kov-aa)
utopenec – *thick spicy sausages* (oo-top-en-ets)
veprove rizek – *pork schnitzel* (vep-rsho-vey zhree-zek)

Emergencies (dial 155 for emergency medical help)

chemist – lekarna (ley-kaarr-na)
doctor – lekar (ley-kaashr)
embassy – ambasada (am-ba-saa-da)
help – pomoc! (pom-ots)
hospital – (nemocnice (nem-ots-nyi-tse)
lost -ztraceny (stratt-senn-ee)
pain – bolest (boll-est)
police – policie (pol-it-see-e)
stolen – ukradny (oo-krad-nee)
toothache – boleni zubu (boh-le-nyee zoo-boooo)

BASIC USEFUL PHRASES

hello/good day – dobry den (dob-ree-den)
goodbye – nashledanou (na-sle-da no)
thank you – dekuju (dyek-oo-yoo)
can we pay please – platit prosim (platt-yit pro-seem)
change money – vymenit penize (vi-myen-yit pe-nyee-ze)
do you have a room free – mate nejaky pokoj volno? (maa-te
    nye-ja-kee po-koy vol-no)
do you speak English – mluvite anglicky? (mloo-vee-te ang-
    lits-ki)
how much is the .../room/...? – kolik stoji pokoj? (ko-lik stoh-

yee po-koy)
please (also used reciprocally, i.e. when a beer is served) –
     prosim (pro-seem)
where is the .../brewery/ – kde je pivovar? (g'de ye piv-o-varr)
which beers have you got – jaka piva mate (ya-kaa pi-va
     maa-te)
which brewery is this beer from? – z ktereho pivovaru prijde
     toto pivo? (skte-re-ho piv-o-va-roo pshri-de to-to piv-o)

GENERAL TERMS

arrival – prizezd (pshree-yezd)
bus – autobus (a-oo-to-booss)
bus station – autobusova stanice (a-oo-to-booss-oh-vay
     sta-nyi-tse)
bridge – most (with short o as in lost)
castle – hrad (hrrad) or zamek (zaa-mek)
departure - odjezd (od-yest)
no – ne
post office – posta (posh-ta)
railway station – nadrazi (naa-dra-zhee)
room – pokoj (pok-oy)
     (outside Prague, the German for B&B is often used in signs
     – zimmerfrei)
stamps – znamky (znaam-kee)
street – ulice (oo-li-tse)
square – namesti (naa-myes-tyee)
ticket (travel) - jizdenka (yeez-denk-a)
train – vlak
tram – tramvaj (tram-vai)
yes – ano, jo (a-no, yo)

NUMBERS 1-10

1 – jeden (yed-enn).
2 – dva.
3 - tri (tshri).
4 – (ctyri (shti-zhri).
5 - pet.(pyet)
6 – sest (shest).
7 – sedm (sed-umm).
8 – osm (oss-umm).
9 – devet (dev-yet).
10 – deset (dess-ett).

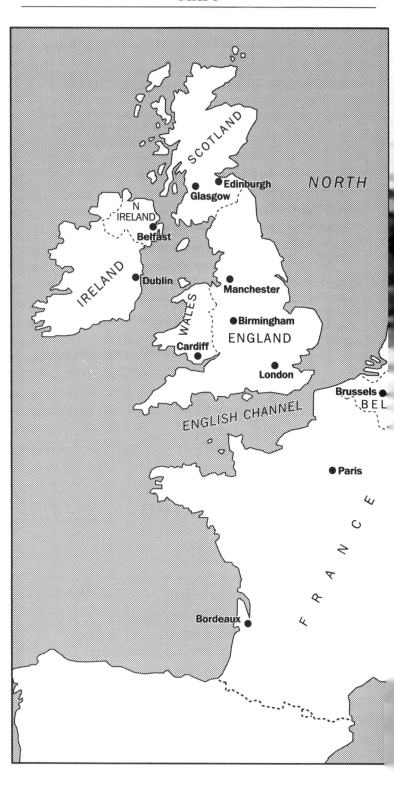

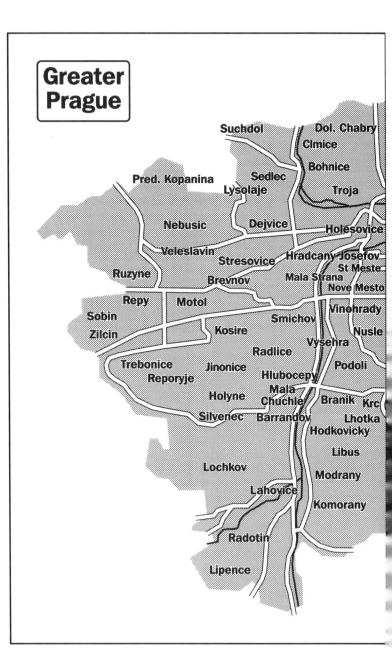

140

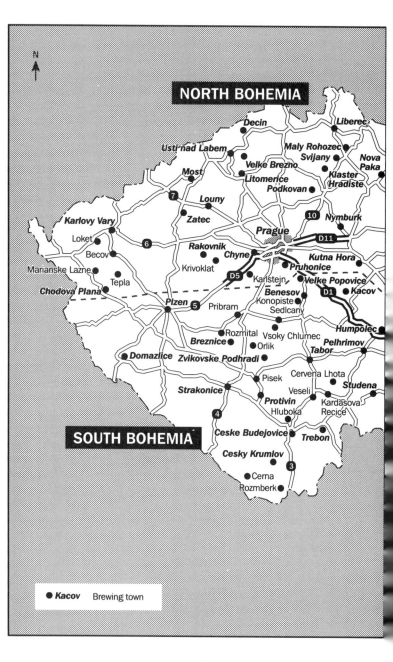

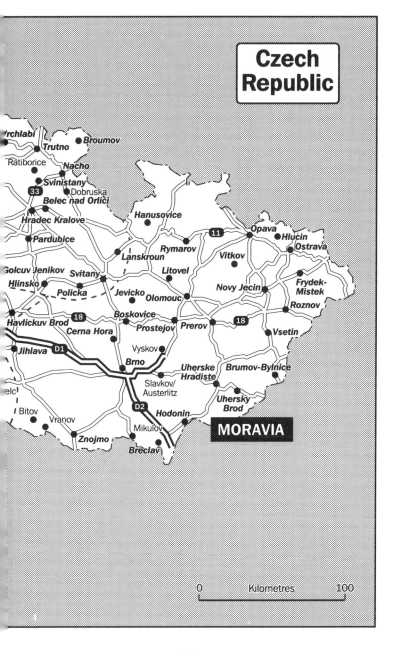

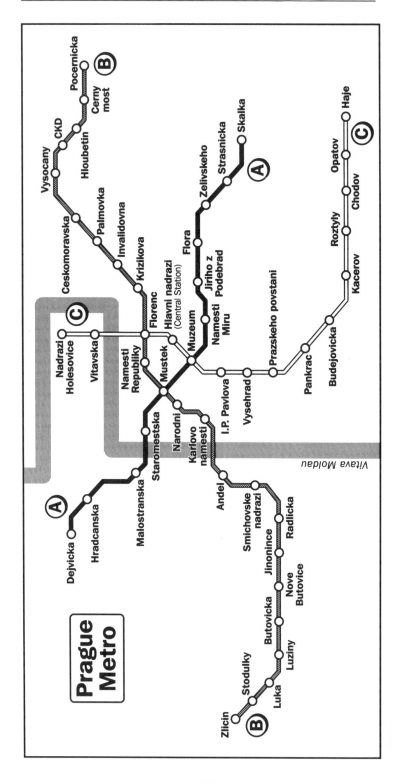

JOIN CAMRA

If you like good beer and good pubs you could be helping to fight to preserve, protect and promote them. CAMRA was set up in the early seventies to fight against the mass destruction of a part of Britain's heritage.

The giant brewers are still pushing through takeovers, mergers and closures of their smaller regional rivals. They are still trying to impose national brands of beer and lager on their customers whether they like it or not, and they are still closing down town and village pubs or converting them into grotesque 'theme' pubs.

CAMRA wants to see genuine free competition in the brewing industry, fair prices, and, above all, a top quality product brewed by local breweries in accordance with local tastes, and served in pubs that maintain the best features of a tradition that goes back centuries.

As a CAMRA member you will be able to enjoy generous discounts on CAMRA products and receive the highly rated monthly newspaper *What's Brewing*. You will be given the CAMRA members' handbook and be able to join in local social events and brewery trips.

To join, complete the form below and, if you wish, arrange for direct debit payments by filling in the form overleaf and returning it to CAMRA. To pay by credit card, contact the membership secretary on (01727) 867201.

Full membership £12; Joint (living partners') membership £14; Life membership £144/£168

Please delete as appropriate:

I/We wish to become members of CAMRA.

I/We agree to abide by the memorandum and articles of association of the company.

I/We enclose a cheque/p.o. for £   (payable to CAMRA Ltd.)

Name(s)

Address

Signature(s)

CAMRA Ltd., 230 Hatfield Road, St Albans, Herts AL1 4LW

INSTRUCTIONS TO YOUR BANK TO PAY DIRECT DEBITS

Please complete parts 1 to 4 to instruct your bank to make payments directly from your account.

Return the form to Campaign for Real Ale, 230 Hatfield Road, St Albans, Herts AL1 4LW.

To the Manager

Bank

1 Please write the full postal address of your bank branch in the box.

2 Name(s) of account holder(s)

Address

Post Code

3 Account Number

Banks may refuse to accept instructions to pay direct debits from some types of account.

Direct debit instructions should only be addressed to banks in the United Kingdom.

CAMRA Computer Membership No. (for office use only)

Originator's Identification No.

| 9 | 2 | 6 | 1 | 2 | 9 |

4 Your instructions to the bank, and signature.

- I instruct you to pay direct debits from my account at the request of Campaign for Real Ale Limited.
- The amounts are variable and are to be debited annually.
- I understand that Campaign for Real Ale Limited may change the amount only after giving me prior notice.
- PLEASE CANCEL ALL PREVIOUS STANDING ORDER INSTRUCTIONS IN FAVOUR OF CAMPAIGN FOR REAL ALE LIMITED.
- I will inform the bank in writing if I wish to cancel this instruction.
- I understand that if any direct debit is paid which breaks the terms of this instruction, the bank will make a refund.

Signature(s)

Date

CAMRA BOOKS

The CAMRA Books range of guides helps you search out the best in beer (and cider) and brew it at home too!

BUYING IN THE UK

All our books are available through bookshops in the UK. If you can't find a book, simply order it from your bookshop using the ISBN number, title and author details given below. CAMRA members should refer to their regular monthly newspaper *What's Brewing* for the latest details and member special offers. CAMRA books are also available by mail-order (postage free) from: CAMRA Books, 230 Hatfield Road, St Albans, Herts, AL1 4LW. Cheques made payable to CAMRA Ltd. Telephone your credit card order on 01727 867201.

BUYING OUTSIDE THE UK

CAMRA books are also sold in many book and beer outlets in the USA and other English-speaking countries. If you have trouble locating a particular book, use the details below to order by mail or fax (+44 1727 867670).

Carriage of £3.00 per book (Europe) and £6.00 per book (US, Australia, New Zealand and other overseas) is charged.

UK BOOKSELLERS

Call CAMRA Books for distribution details and book list. CAMRA Books are listed on all major CD-ROM book lists and on our Internet site: http://www.cityscape.co.uk/users/al96/beer/html

OVERSEAS BOOKSELLERS

Call or fax CAMRA Books for details of local distributors.

Distributors are required for some English language territories. Rights enquiries (for non-English language editions) should be addressed to the managing editor.

Good Beer Guides

These are comprehensive guides researched by professional beer writers and CAMRA enthusiasts. Use these guides to find the best beer on your travels or to plan your itinerary for the finest drinking. Travel and accommodation information, plus maps, help you on your way and there's plenty to read about the history of brewing, the beer styles and the local cuisine to back up the entries for bars and beverages.

bars, beer halls and gardens, and the food to match. You'll also find all the background information for the world's most famous beer extravaganza, the Munich Oktoberfest.

Author Graham Lees, a founder member of CAMRA, has lived and worked in Munich for several years and has endlessly toured Bavaria in search of the perfect pint.

Use the following code to order this book from your bookshop: ISBN 1-85249-114-0

Good Beer Guide to Munich and Bavaria

by Graham Lees

206 pages   Price: £8.99

A fifth of the world's breweries – some 750 – are located in the region covered by this guide. The beers have rich, deep flavours and aromas and are generously hopped. You will find dark lagers, wheat beers, members of the ale family, wonderfully quenching and refreshing beers that have become cult drinks. The guide tells you where to find the best beers and the many splendid

Good Beer Guide to Belgium and Holland

by Tim Webb

286 pages   Price: £9.99

Discover the stunning range and variety of beers available in the Low Countries, our even nearer neighbours via Le Tunnel. There are such revered styles as Trappist Ales, fruit beers, wheat beers and the lambic and gueuze specialities made by the centuries-old method of spontaneous fermentation.

Channel-hopping Tim Webb's latest edition of the

guide offers even more bars in which an incredible array of beers can be enjoyed. If you are going on holiday to this region then you'll find details of travel, accommodation, food, beer museums, brewery visits and festivals, as well as guides to the cafés, beer shops and warehouses you can visit. There are maps, tasting notes, beer style guide and a beers index to complete the most comprehensive companion to drinking with your Belgian and Dutch hosts.

Use the following code to order this book from your bookshop: ISBN 1-85249-115-9

GOOD BEER GUIDE
edited by Jeff Evans

546 pages   Price: £10.99

Fancy a pint? Let CAMRA's *Good Beer Guide* lead the way. Revised each year to include around 5,000 great pubs serving excellent ale – country pubs, town pubs and pubs by the sea.

The guide includes information about meals, accommodation, family rooms, no-smoking areas and much more.

Fully and freshly researched by members of the Campaign for Real Ale, real enthusiasts who use the pubs week in, week out. No payment is ever taken for inclusion. The guide has location maps for each county and you can read full details of all Britain's breweries (big and small) and the ales they produce, including tasting notes. CAMRA's Good Beer Guide is still Britain's best value pub guide – a must for anyone who loves beer and pubs.

KNOWN GEMS & HIDDEN TREASURES – A POCKET GUIDE TO THE PUBS OF LONDON
by Peter Haydon

224 pages   Price: £7.99

If you live in or visit London, then you need this guide in your top pocket! It will take you to the well-known and historic pubs you must not miss, but also to the pubs which are tucked away and which locals keep to themselves.

The grass roots organisation of CAMRA and beer journalist Peter Haydon have brought London's pubs alive through their descriptions of ale, food, entertainment, history and architecture. These pubs have a story to tell.

The pubs in this pocket, portable, guide are listed by locality with a street address and London postal code districts heading pages so that you can easily match your location with the nearest pub. The guide covers pubs which are near tube and railway stations and gives relevant bus route numbers. It covers central London out to the commuter belts of Bushey and Surbiton.

Use the following code to order this book from your bookshop: ISBN 1-85249-118-3

CAMRA GUIDES

Painstakingly researched and checked, these guides are the leaders in their field, bringing you to the door of pubs which serve real ale and more…

GOOD PUB FOOD
by Susan Nowak

448 pages   Price: £9.99

The pubs in these pages serve food as original and exciting as anything available in far more expensive restaurants. And, as well as the exotic and unusual, you will find landlords and landladies serving simple, nourishing pub fare such as a genuine ploughman's lunch or a steak and kidney pudding.

You'll discover cooking from a new wave of young chefs who would prefer to run a pub than a restaurant. Many pubs are producing the traditional dishes of their regions, building smokeries, keeping cattle and goats, growing vegetables and herbs, creating vibrant, modern cuisine from fresh ingredients. Recipes from some of them are dotted about this guide so you can

try them at home.
Award-winning food and beer writer Susan Nowak, who has travelled the country to complete this fourth edition of the guide, says that 'eating out' started in British inns and taverns and this guide is a contribution to an appreciation of all that is best in British food…and real cask conditioned ale.

Use the following code to order this book from your bookshop: ISBN 1-85249-116-7

ROOM AT THE INN
by Jill Adam

242 pages   Price: £8.99

From the first pub claiming to have sold Stilton cheese to travellers in 1720 to old smugglers haunts in Dorset, *Room at the Inn* gives details of pubs up and down the country offering generous hospitality. Travellers and tourists looking for a traditional British alternative to bland impersonal hotels need look no further than this guide.

The guide contains almost 350 inns – plus some hotels and motels – which provide overnight accommodation and a wholesome English breakfast. Some have been welcoming visitors for centuries. You'll also find a good pint of real ale on your arrival. To help you further there are maps, information on pub meals, family facilities, local tourist attractions and much more. Room at the Inn is a must for the glove compartment of the family car and vital reading for anyone planning a bed and breakfast break, sports tour or business trip.

Use the following code to order this book from your bookshop: ISBN 1-85249-119-1

GUIDE TO REAL CIDER
by Ted Bruning

256 pages   Price: £7.99

Cider is making a major comeback and Real Cider is worth seeking out wherever you are. This guide helps you find one of Britain's oldest, tastiest and most fascinating drinks. Cider has been made in Britain since before Roman times. But most cider you find in pubs today has been pasteurised, with carbon dioxide added. The resulting drink bears little resemblance to the full-flavoured taste of traditional Real Cider. Reading this guide makes your mouth water as you leaf through details of more than 2000 pubs selling the real stuff. There are also many farmhouse producers from all over the country and outlets for Cider's equally drinkable cousin, Perry – if you bring a container. Some will even sell you a container! Author Ted Bruning is the editor of the Cider Press, a quarterly supplement to What's Brewing, CAMRA's national newspaper. He has collated information from all over the UK to give you a taste of this fine traditional drink. So why not join him and savour a wealth of different flavours?

Use the following code to order this book from your bookshop: ISBN 1-85249-117-5

BREW YOUR OWN

Learn the basics of brewing real ales at home from the experts. And then move on to more ambitious recipes which imitate well-loved ales from the UK and Europe.

GUIDE TO HOME BREWING

by Graham Wheeler

240 pages   Price: £6.99

The best way to learn successful home-brewing basics is over the shoulder of expert Graham Wheeler, in this second edition of his popular guide. Find out how to brew ales, stouts, lagers and wheat beers from kits, malt extract and full mash. If some of this jargon is new to you then read on… Equipment, ingredients, yeast, water, boiling and cooling, fermenting, finishing, bottling, kits, measurements and calculations. These are just some of the subjects fully covered in this definitive beginner's guide to home brewing. There are also many classic recipes with which to try out your new-found skills. The perfect gift for the home-brewer in your life!

Use the following code to order this book from your bookshop: ISBN 1-85249-112-4

BREW YOUR OWN REAL ALE AT HOME
by Graham Wheeler and Roger Protz

196 pages   Price: £6.99

This book is a treasure chest for all real ale fans and home brew enthusiasts. It contains recipes which allow you to replicate some famous cask-conditioned beers at home or to customise brews to your own particular taste. The authors have examined the ingredients and brewing styles of well-known ales and have gleaned important information from brewers, with and without their co-operation. Computer-aided guesswork and an expert palate have filled in the gaps where the brewers would reveal no more.

As well as the recipes, the brewing process is explained along with the equipment required, all of which allows you to brew beer using wholly natural ingredients. Detailed recipes and instructions are given along with tasting notes for each ale. Conversion details are given so that the measurements can be used world-wide.

Use the following code to order this book from your bookshop: ISBN 1-85249-113-2

BREW CLASSIC EUROPEAN BEERS AT HOME
by Graham Wheeler and Roger Protz

196 pages   Price: £8.99

Keen home brewers can now recreate some of the world's classic beers. In your own home you can brew superb pale ales, milds, porters, stouts, Pilsners, Alt, Kolsch, Trappist, wheat beers, sour beers, even the astonishing fruit lambics of Belgium… and many more.

Graham Wheeler and his computer have teamed up with Roger Protz and his unrivalled knowledge of brewing and beer styles. Use the detailed recipes and information about ingredients to imitate the cream of international beers. Discover the role played by ingredients, yeasts and brewing equipment and procedure in these well-known drinks. Measurements are given in UK, US and European units, emphasising the truly international scope of the beer styles within.

Use the following code to order this book from your bookshop: ISBN 1-85249-117-5

Please tick the book(s) you require and total your enclosed payment below. Please send this form to CAMRA Books, 230 Hatfield Road, St Albans, Herts, AL1 4LW.

Good Beer Guide to Munich and Bavaria	£8.99	☐
Good Beer Guide to Belgium and Holland	£8.99	☐
Known Treasures and Hidden Gems – London Pubs	£7.99	☐
Good Cider Guide	£7.99	☐
Good Pub Food	£9.99	☐
Room at the Inn	£8.99	☐
Guide to Home Brewing	£6.99	☐
Brew Your Own Real Ale at Home	£6.99	☐
Brew Classic European Beers at Home	£8.99	☐

Total £ enclosed:

I enclose a cheque made payable to CAMRA Ltd/I'd like to pay by credit card.

Credit card number:

Expiry date:

Signature:

Name

Address

Post code

Telephone number